Saying "I Do" in Paradise

Saying "I Do" in Paradise

by Jean Stewart Berg

Aventine Press

For Richard, my best man.

Table of Contents

Introduction

Paradise? I know paradise; I'm a theologian, for heaven's sake. But paradise can be more than biblical; our paradise even has a zip code. Home for us is the tropical island of Cozumel, 13 miles offshore from Mexico's Yucatan Peninsula: now that's paradise.

The island's original Mayan name was *Cuzimil,* "the island of swallows" for the thousands of swallows that stopped here on their long journey from the north to Cuba each year. The island was discovered on May 3, 1518, by the Spaniard Juan de Grivalva who sailed from Cuba. Hernán Cortés followed the next year, using the island as a base from which to attack Indians living on the mainland. To the surprise of the Spaniards, the island was already inhabited and developed. Mayan-speaking natives had created a small village, now El Cedral, with streets and properties defined by colorfully painted fences. The first mass on Mexican territory was offered in El Cedral. One of the lasting gifts Cortes brought to Cuzimil was an array of diseases imported from Europe that nearly decimated the island's population.

Today, a dozen or so families make El Cedral their home, but in honor of the first explorer's arrival, each May a huge festival swells the population to several thousand for four days of fiesta in the Mexican tradition. Games, livestock exhibits, dancing and music, regionally made crafts, and traditional foods, plus the requisite bullfight and horse race, make El Cedral at fiesta time a destination worthy of any modern-day explorer. In the time of de Grivalva and Cortes, this *pueblo* was a five-mile hike from the water's edge through jungle crowded with sturdy vines and many creatures large and small that go bump in the night. Now, a paved road lets the traveler arrive in comfort and safety.

Cozumel is about 189 square miles; head to toe, it's 29 miles long and across the middle, nine miles wide. There is small danger of altitude sickness: the highest point reaches only 50 feet into the skies. Surrounding the land, especially on the south and west sides, are some of the world's most dazzling reefs; fish love us. And the nearly two million tourists that arrive each year love the fish. Oh, yes, I nearly forgot: In addition to El Cedral, we have one town, San Miguel, which has a few major streets and eight traffic lights.

I discovered this island paradise before it had a zip code. In 1976, I ran for the U.S. Congress, running for a seat as a Missouri Representative. I was part of lively and often significant debates that opened new lines of public discourse, but in the end, I lost. So I flew to Florida on an impulse to join my good friend, Sandy, for a women's conference that I thought would lift my spirits and remind me that there were still important events where I, and other women like me, could have a voice. At the conclusion of the conference, Sandy and I noticed a small ad in the weekend travel section of the local newspaper offering a promotional trip to a small Mexican island called Cozumel. The total cost for round-trip airfare? $29.00. How could we resist? Why *would* we?

As our plane touched down at the airport with its one runway, we knew we would reap a big return on our $29.00 investment. There were a few small hotels in San Miguel, but we found an obliging taxi driver who delivered us to the one hotel on the north beach. It had two stories, about 26 rooms, a photo-op perfect white sandy beach and, for dining, an open *palapa,* a palm-thatched umbrella-like structure that rises out of the sand to provide shade. Absolutely perfect. Because we would only be staying for the weekend, accommodations were scarce, and we didn't have reservations, this hotel was perfect for our budgets and our schedule.

Our explorations that weekend revealed tall coconut palm trees that provided shade from the midday sun and colorful hibiscus that lined the walkways. Mexico's glorious bougainvillea – also called *paper flower*—climbed recklessly up the walls and around the hotel grounds. Wherever we turned, we saw floral greetings in purple, magenta, yellow, coral, lemon, and red. Even the iguanas sunning themselves in the midday heat smiled. The clear water, aqua blue-green and fresh as a Colorado trout stream, could not be the same water I knew as a child in California on the Pacific coast or in any of the other places I traveled. Little yellow and black and red and polka dot fish alternately drifted, then zoomed past our knees as we stood in the shallow water.

One morning, I was awakened by the sound of music; looking out from our balcony, I discovered a young man seated on a rock beyond the shore, playing a Bach fugue on his wood flute. The sky behind him was so blue, the clouds so white, and the sunshine so bright that I recognized paradise immediately, not the paradise I had learned about in Sunday School but a paradise I felt in that moment.

The following year, my husband, Dick, returned to Cozumel with me. Many years and many trips later, we celebrated our twenty-fifth wedding anniversary overlooking the same sea. We invited friends who had been part of our wedding party 25 years earlier to join us and together we returned to the hotel Sandy and I had discovered earlier. Progress had come to Cozumel; a nine-floor tower had sprung up next to the two-story building where we had originally stayed. Our rooms were on the eighth floor overlooking the same beautiful clear waters. The tower already showed signs of island life: salt-induced corrosion in the elevator system encouraged us to walk the many steps rather than risk being captive in a rusty elevator.

Now that I write and participate in so many weddings and anniversary celebrations and renewals of vows I realize the opportunity we missed; we never considered a ceremony. But long walks on the beach in the early morning, breakfasts spent tossing small pieces of toast to the waiting fish, and late-night dinners under the stars while we reminisced about the years of our marriage made the time pass too quickly. And it was perfect.

Cozumel still had no zip code, but it was growing gradually. It called to us. And we had discovered a church in Cancun, where we often stayed on our vacations. Cancun was Cozumel's more sophisticated younger sibling with its fast-paced, fast-food development of high-rise, high-cost condominiums and hotels, each more elegant than the former. We were drawn to *La Iglesia Presbiteriana Puerto del*

Cielo or the Gate of Heaven Presbyterian Church and made it our church home when we were in Cancun. Minister Ramón Celis became our Mexican pastor and good friend. When Ramón's ministries moved to Cozumel, he encouraged us to join him, "Come to Cozumel; the church needs you." We made our decision with no specific plan for why or how the church needed us.

We answered Cozumel's call to make the beautiful island our home on Sunday, February 16, 1998, willingly trading the white snow of St. Louis, Missouri, for the white sand of Cozumel. I remember the day not only because it was my birthday, but because before we finished unpacking our two-door, very fully packed car, Ramón stopped by with a warm greeting and a request. People had expressed a wish for worship services in English. Would I preach the following Sunday morning? Eben-Ezer Presbyterian Church had a long history of community service and an open policy toward many needs on the island of Cozumel so this was no real surprise. Caught up in the euphoria of arrival, I said "Sure, I'll try." That rising clamor for an English-language worship was a barely heard whisper; one person appeared!

While an attempt had been made to organize a congregation, it was uneven and frail. Over time, however, we did create and nurture a small interdenominational congregation of people who sought an English-language worship service. As I write this, we are in our ninth year. We are a glorious mix: Catholic, Methodist, United Church of Christ, Baptist, Presbyterian, Unitarian, United Church of Canada, Jewish, and whoever else appears. We worship weekly at Eben-Ezer, and I am designated by the *Consistorio*—the governing body of the church— as the minister of worship.

We were just settling into our new life in Mexico, living in a bed and breakfast close to the center of San Miguel, when a couple arrived for a week's stay at the same B&B. The owners assured them I could perform their wedding, and in the absence of any likely alternative, I agreed. The bride and groom, their parents, and friends all actively participated in the planning and oversight of every detail. At a rehearsal dinner planned by their friends, I was uncertain about where the groom should stand. His mother asked me, "Are you sure you know what you are doing?" And for a moment I wondered, too. All went according to plan, however. On a quiet beach at sunset, children handed out programs to each guest and a very happy bride and groom spoke their "I do's" in paradise.

As I've now married more than 500 couples on this beautiful tropical island of Cozumel, I've done a lot of thinking about weddings, about how they have changed since my husband Dick and I married in a church in San Marino, California, 50 years ago. And the ways they haven't changed. And the difference between getting married and being married, the difference between the fairy-tale wedding and the real-life job of marriage. This book not only represents what I've thought about, it also tells the stories of many of the brides and grooms who have stood before me and pledged to take on that job. I hope you'll learn from my experience, whether you're a bride, a groom, a parent, or a minister or someone who likes to read about weddings. Enjoy reading how others have created the weddings they've always dreamed of and enjoyed the ones that didn't turn out according to plan.

Destination Weddings

Getting married away from home almost always brings surprises for the bride, the groom, the family, or the guests. And often for all of them. Sometimes, I'm the one who is surprised. A couple from the Philippines booked a wedding at the island's premier Hotel El Presidente. They were alone without the family and friends usually expected at a wedding. I wrote a special greeting to accommodate the small gathering, which would include the hotel representative and my husband, Dick, as a witness:

"We stand here in the sight of God to witness and to celebrate and to bless the joining together of Juan and Elisa in holy marriage. Although we are few, you are not alone. You are surrounded with our prayers and we share in your joy. This is a very special day."

It turned out that the day was more special than I knew. When Dick and I arrived, we found 100 chairs set up facing the sea and ta-

bles decorated with beautiful tropical flowers, candles, crystal, and silver. There were guests everywhere.

How had I made such a mistake? It came down to the difference between a wedding guest and a hotel guest. The bride and groom were staying at the hotel so when I asked how many guests, the person from the hotel said, "Just two." The wedding guests arrived for the wedding day by cruise ship. As the many bridesmaids and groomsmen assembled, I stood at the bar revising my notes, making several changes as the string quartet gentled the guests to their seats. The guests included a priest whom I invited to offer the blessing. It turns out he intended to do just that all along.

Not long ago the words *destination* and *wedding* were not an item. There were *destinations,* and there were *weddings.* Now married, they are a noun. And they are a trendy couple. *Destination weddings* reflect the growing affluence of young professionals, the diminishing role of tradition in families and rituals, and the smart marketing that appeals to couples looking for something different. Many couples are distanced from their communities of worship, if indeed they have them. The rabbi, priest, or minister who couples asked to marry them in the past are not as central to the lives of couples getting married today. On a more positive note, travel and the rapid and visual communications offered by technology like the Internet have opened new vistas, introduced new possibilities. With beautiful photos of wedding couples, scenes of sandy white beaches, and dazzling sunsets reflecting over the water like a Monet painting, it is more than attractive; it's absolutely irresistible.

Destinations vary from city parks to mountain lakes to sandswept beaches, sites that hold special places in the hearts of the bride and groom or appeal to adventurous spirits. There are couples who want to exchange vows and rings in parachutes high in the sky or under the sea with fish as their witnesses. I don't go there. But almost always, the wedding couple seeks to blend the new setting with traditional words, often modified but still recognizable.

Over my years living in the paradise that is Cozumel, I have allowed myself to be swept up by the "destination weddings" rush of the present times. And to tell the truth, I love it! This is how I think about destination weddings: every wedding can be a happy and holy moment. Every wedding can be a spiritual and sacred moment. A bride and groom barefoot on the beach and surrounded by the sights and the sounds of the sea are as beautiful as the wedding couple standing at the church altar in their hometown. It is the intentions of the bride and groom and those who stand with them (barefoot or shod) that make the ceremony sacred. As the minister, my most important task is to listen to the dreams and visions of the couple getting married and carefully shape them into a ceremony of substance and joy.

Susan and Greg were friends of a Denver friend of mine; they were Jewish (Susan), and Catholic (Greg). The wedding planning began with the site: a remote six-room inn south of the ancient Mayan city, Tulum, which is 60 miles south of the fast-paced and trendy Cancun. My Colorado friend assured them that I lived near Cancun and they might want me to officiate at the wedding.

As it turned out, simple though it may have seemed at the beginning, nothing about the wedding was simple. First, I explained that to travel that distance on a Saturday afternoon would make it difficult for me to be home on the island for Sunday morning worship. I would need to travel by ferry, bus, and taxi just to arrive at the wedding site. But I would gladly seek someone to lead the ceremony for them. That someone would, ideally, be twins: a rabbi and a priest. Impossible.

Then, thought I, since we're not going to get the ideal, perhaps a rabbi or a priest. Impossible. Priests do not offer the sacrament of marriage outside the church and the closest rabbi is in Mexico City, 2,000 miles away. So, in the absence of one or the other, I agreed to write and officiate their wedding ceremony. I was so happy I did!

Dick accompanied me across the channel by ferry, south by bus to Tulum, to the wedding site by taxi. We arrived mid-afternoon for the sunset wedding. The month was May; the day was warm with a gentle breeze, the water clear and inviting. The little inn was filled with Susan and Greg's 10 wedding guests. Some were still swimming, others taking sun, some just talking under palm trees. It was pure tranquility and delight. Tropical flowers growing nearby became the bride's bouquet, other flowers were woven into colorful hair ornaments, still other flowers made an aisle on the sand for Susan to walk.

I had prepared the ceremony with some guidance from them: "Please make this a spiritual ceremony celebrating our two traditions."

The ceremony was not long but guests were attentive, and Susan and Greg spoke their vows with a calm conviction that I believe will sustain their marriage for all their years.

Planning the Destination Wedding

Long-distance wedding planning can begin with easy access through the Internet or a community library. Beware that it takes time and attention to detail to plan a wedding in a place you've never been and may not go to until the time of the wedding it-self.

Hundreds of weddings are performed on Cozumel every year. Most Mexicans marry in a civil ceremony (with a judge) that may be or may not be followed by a religious ceremony (or the church ceremony may come years later). Foreigners coming to Mexico often marry in a religious/spiritual ceremony but having a civil ceremony here is not the easy event many imagine. Civil ceremonies require lots of documents the Mexicans seem to love. Time is required to translate the application, provide documents and blood tests and register witnesses, and then for the application to be processed by the Mexican government. Somewhere, there is a rumor floating in space that it's easy to get a "quickie" wedding in Mexico (also a "quickie" divorce). Not so. The one judge on our island has told of many Americans who arrive in his office at the *Palacio Municipal* saying they want to be married. "When?" he asks. "Maybe around three o'clock" they reply. And the judge just stares. "Impossible!" he assures them.

If you are reading this while planning a destination wedding, I urge you to find out what the process is in the country in which you plan to marry. It may be far easier to have the civil ceremony in the country in which you live and have what most consider "the real wedding" in the destination of your choice. Then you can experience the beauty of a wedding seeking the blessing of God, making sacred lifetime promises, and receiving the blessing of family and friends without the worry and work of a civil ceremony in a foreign country.

It takes a lot of courage and trust to plan a destination wedding. As you plan your destination wedding, don't forget what the most important element is: the wedding. Consider together the weddings you remember. What gave them special meaning? What are your own beliefs about the importance of the wedding ceremony? Who is it for? These are questions for the couple getting married to consider no matter where they get married.

Usually—but not always—the destination is known by the couple, but those with whom all arrangements are entrusted are strangers. Even when all the arrangements are set, things can still go awry. For those reasons, couples should be well-fortified with flexibility in addition to trust and courage. Jose and Stacy managed all of that on their wedding day. The day dawned sunny and beautiful, exactly as hoped for. However, as the wedding hour approached, the sky darkened and a wind began to blow. The wedding could still have gone as planned—a dark sky often offers a beautiful sunset. But the groom arrived an hour late and so did the floral arch. And the family members arriving by plane.

Just as everyone thought we were back on schedule, the wind blew the floral arch to the ground and we were in darkness because the sun had set. I needed a flashlight to read and wedding photos were almost impossible. But Stacy, Jose, their family, and guests found much to treasure, including hearing the scripture, 1 Corinthians 13, read by the mother of the bride in English and the mother of the groom in Spanish.

Tips

If you're thinking of getting married in a foreign place, remember these tips:

1. Do your research. How will you find musicians? Can they sing and play what you want? What about a photographer? Florist? Etc., etc., etc.
2. Use a wedding planner in the location where you will be married.
3. Consider the setting as you make your plans. For example, music played in a house of worship on a full pipe organ does not translate easily to strings on the beach.
4. Have a back-up plan. What about the weather? Cruise ships with wedding guests and sometimes the bride and groom are known to divert their port of call and wedding parties destined for Cozumel have been known to tie up in Jamaica! Or the other way around.

5. Learn to trust people you don't know or take a scouting trip. Or do both. I've married many couples I met only a day or two before the wedding. I always hope to meet with the couple prior to the wedding day, but often e-mail is our way to communicate. When couples arrive by cruise ship, we meet for the first time at the ceremony. That is my least favorite way. (See Appendix Two for the form I ask each couple to complete prior to their arrival). Ask yourself if you are able to work with someone you don't know.

6. Expect the unexpected. What will you do if the plane delivering all the flowers to all the florists for the entire island is delayed? Will you be able to enjoy the ceremony without flowers? Can you make a back-up plan? A wedding planner can help with all of these possibilities.

These are only a few of the elements in a destination wedding that can go awry. It's a good idea to make sure that you are ready for the unexpected and able to accept it Honestly, every wedding is memorable and unique. The problem may come if a couple expects perfection to conform to their exact fantasy. In my years of marrying people, I've found that all weddings are perfect. Even when they aren't.

So hold on to your veil and grab your top hat and come with me for a tour of what a wedding in paradise takes.

Why Get Married

Some couples have strength and courage I can only imagine. Ken and Mariliz met in 2001 in New York City where both lived and worked. On his wedding day, Ken showed me photos of his two young sons and said how much they loved Mariliz and she them. On September 11, Mariliz was working her craft as a fiber-optics technician not at a computer as usual, but high atop a telephone pole close to the World Trade Center. So close, in fact, that the two planes flew no more than 50 feet overhead before crashing into the Twin Towers. Mariliz jumped from the pole into the waiting arms of rescue workers. The jump shattered her leg into four pieces and caused other injuries as well. The prognosis for full recovery, the doctors said, was "impossible. She will most likely never walk again." The road back to independent mobility was slow and painful; Ken was at Mariliz's side every moment. He cooked for her;

bathed, carried, and cared for her for nearly a
year. Now they were ready to make complete in
the sight of God the commitment they shared.
As he told me this story before the ceremony,
Ken looked at me with tears in his eyes and
said, "I love her so much."

I stood with Ken on the beach as he waited
for Mariliz. Accompanied by the gentle sound of
waves for music, Mariliz walked, without any
visible limitation, across the sand. Wearing a
simple white sheath dress, with neither jewelry
nor flowers, she was radiant. Ken reached out
and took her hand; I felt like an intruder. The
ceremony was short but sweet and so real.
They needed nothing more.

Rituals help shape our lives just as our life
experience creates ritual. From the early years of the
child kneeling at a bedside in evening prayer through
the final goodbyes at the end of life, we express our
beliefs and our very being through ritual. To be
called by name is an essential and precious part
of a ritual, making each person a significant part
of the ritual. I name the bride and groom at many
points in the wedding ceremony; this is their ritual.
Rituals are life-giving; they connect us to our past
and those we love. You may not be surprised to learn
that I love rituals, the continuity they provide, the

memories they evoke. I love being part of creating new rituals and, when it is a good idea, discarding the old. I love combining traditions. For example, in the past few years, as either the bride or groom or both bring children into the marriage, I have built words of welcome and love for the children into the ceremony. Part of this ritual may include the parents presenting the children with a special gift—a symbol of their unity. This part of the ceremony is often included after the rings are exchanged by the bride and groom. You will find other rituals included in this volume as well (see Appendix One). I do not love dogma. I do not love the rigid and often judgmental results that dogma invites. For me, ritual is the sweet nectar and dogma the bitter.

Weddings are a precious ritual. Each wedding is unique; within the generous bounds of tradition, the bride and groom fulfill their long-held dreams. The setting, the guests, the words read and spoken, the prayers offered, the blessings, all form a ceremony that is uniquely the creation of the marrying couple.

As I stand before those marrying couples, I often wish we had more than one word for love. The English language is impoverished by this lack. We don't love pizza the same as we love our dearest friend, partner, or spouse, but we use the same word. The same holds true with the Bible in English. Biblical Greek does at least offer a modest cafeteria of choices (*philia,* meaning love of friends and humankind; *eros,* from which we take the word "erotic;" and *agape,* holy spiritual love). The challenge comes when "eros" is the only love the marrying couple is interested in and the minister is reading "agape." Not the same. When reading scripture, I always encourage couples to think of love beyond the romance of the moment. It's understandably a grand hope.

A scripture I often suggest comes from the Book of 1 John, beginning with chapter 4 verse 7:

"Beloved, let us love one another, because love is from God; everyone who loves is born of God and knows God...for God is love...God's love was revealed among us in this way: God sent God's only child into the world so that we might live through him. In this is love; not that we loved God but that God loved us...No one has ever seen God; if we love one another, God lives in us, and God's love is perfected in us."

Many people ask, "Why get married at all? It's only a piece of paper..." Over time, I have come to value weddings far more than I did as a bride. I value the traditions the wedding represents, the bonding, the healing, the honesty, the joy, the new possibilities, the hopes. Little separates the cynical from the spiritual when each stands in the company of friends and families, asking for God's blessing for their marriage and the promises they have come to commit to one another. For most, it is a transforming moment. And the couples are touched, often unexpectedly.

Weddings are one of life's most precious rituals; they bring two people together with all the love that has made them who they are, and together they pledge their futures in love. Whatever journey has brought the couple to this moment, they join their deepest hopes for life together for as long as they live.

It takes courage, trust, and outright audacity to make the profound and really intimate promises for life shared together in the presence of guests, whether few or many. In speaking aloud those familiar words that those speaking have often heard many times, the words shimmer with the radiance of the couples' personal commitment and that makes them special every time: "...I, John, choose you, Susan, to be my wife..."

In many countries, there is a distinct separation between a civil wedding and a religious wedding. Not all couples seek a spiritual blessing and not all couples I marry have deeply held religious beliefs or traditions. There should be a place for both, I believe. For a couple to seek a minister or rabbi or priest just to fulfill a social function is silly at best and hypocritical at worst. Like all human institutions, marriage evolves and changes over time. But I'd bet the farm there will be weddings farther into the future than we can see.

Come to the Wedding

Meet Julie and Jon. They came to Cozumel for their wedding accompanied by Julie's grandfather and her 12-year-old son, Peter, who were the only wedding guests. Peter and his great-grandfather were obviously close. Great-grandpa winked at Peter as Peter escorted his mother down the aisle. Julie wrote about herself and Jon, "…we have been dating for about a year; we met at a time in each of our lives when we both needed tender loving care. We are very good friends and have a lot in common. We are both religious and believe this is God's plan for our lives so we would like the ceremony to have references to love and commitment from the Bible." Peter carried my Bible with great care and reverence during the ceremony. During the prayers, we remembered Julie's grandmother, who had died recently.

Julie and Jon represent many couples who take
the ceremony—and the rituals and words that
comprise the ceremony—seriously. They are a very
religious Christian couple and looked to the Bible for
inspiration. People of other faiths use their sacred
texts while others look to literature and poetry to
deepen the meaning of the ceremony. What matters
is that the marrying couple takes the words and the
ceremony as the sacred, important markers that
they are.

When I greet the couple and their guests, I say,
"Every wedding is a holy and sacred moment. We
do not have to be in a church or house of worship to
ask God's presence. God is present with us here and
now." To me, the challenge and most important task
is to bring together the beauty of a secular setting,
the joy of the long-anticipated occasion, and the
sacredness of what we are saying. Because I write
each ceremony for the couple, sometimes with large
changes and sometimes with small, every wedding
is fresh and new, even after hundreds of weddings.
I still approach each one as though it was the first,
and it feels that way because every couple brings me
something that no other couple can.

Many couples have Hollywood movies running
in their heads when they imagine their weddings.
Recently, a television crew came to Cozumel to film
a couple on their Caribbean honeymoon, and they

began with the wedding ceremony. Chosen from a competition sponsored by a television program in the States, the couple had been married six months. After a week on the island, I "married" them while the crew filmed us. I was asked to "act" only the blessing and exchange of rings and the final blessing. Afterward, they both said to me, "You know, now we feel really married!"

Because we are usually outside on the beach, many guests arrive in a party mood. I'm sure some parents and grandparents feared that we were there to play volleyball in bikinis. Not so. I'm happy to say that most of the couples I have married have approached the ceremony with the dignity and seriousness marriage deserves. And the guests quickly catch the mood of seriousness and joy.

In Their Own Words

When the wedding couple tells me they want to prepare their own vows, I encourage them to do so *in addition* to traditional vows that most wish to speak and guests expect to hear. A copy for me too, please. Just to prompt if necessary. Not insisting on a copy led to this: Bride: "You are the raspberries on my cheesecake. You are the strawberries in my champagne." Groom: stunned silence.

Words carefully chosen and tenderly spoken can give the wedding ceremony its own signature.

I've heard several cut-and-paste vows created and offered as an honest attempt to find words that feel comfortable and a departure from what the couple considers too traditional. I have also heard declarations of love and confessions of failure and infidelity too personal for any but the couple to hear.

Angela and Michael spoke their marriage promises in the company of a few friends and family. Later they shared the readings and wedding photos on their personal website. Michael spoke first and then Angela repeated the same vow to Michael, substituting where necessary:

From this day on I choose you, Angela, to be my wife. I give to you my sacred promise to always stand by your side as your ever-faithful husband, to laugh with you in the good times and struggle with you in the bad. I promise to love you without reservation or judgment, to comfort you in times of distress and encourage you to achieve your dreams. I promise to grow with you in mind and spirit, to cherish you and bring out the best in you always, keeping our love pure with honesty and openness. I will thank God for you and love you from the bottom of my heart, from the depths of my soul, forever.

Readings

The wealth of available writings can enhance the wedding with beauty and depth apart from traditional passages from the Bible. One such reading taken from *The Prophet* by the Lebanese mystic Kahlil Gibran is chosen especially by couples who hold fast to their deep sense of spirituality but eschew traditional religious writings. Now a classic, the small volume of just over 100 pages was first published in 1923. This short dialogue is a good example of a wedding reading that does not come from any religious tradition:

And what of Marriage, master? And he answered
   saying:
You were born together, and together you shall
   be forevermore.
You shall be together when the white wings of
   death scatter your days.
Aye, you shall be together even in the silent
   memory of God.
But let there be spaces in your togetherness;
And let the winds of the heavens dance between
   you.
Love one another, but make not a bond of love:
Let it rather be a moving sea between the shores
   of your souls.
Fill each other's cup, but drink not from one
   cup.

Give one another of your bread, but eat not from
   the same loaf.
Sing and dance together and be joyous, but let
   each one of you be alone,
Even as the strings of a lute are alone though
   they quiver with the same music.
Give your hearts, but not into each other's
   keeping.
For only the hand of Life can contain your
   hearts.
And stand together yet not too near together:
For the pillars of the temple stand apart,
And the oak tree and the cypress grow not in
   each other's shadow.

During my seminary years, I developed a deep
appreciation and affection for Jewish faith and
traditions. Our Jewish daughter-in-law Freddi has
enhanced that appreciation; so much so, our son Scott
has converted. He and Freddi spoke their wedding
vows under the *chupa*, a canopy that symbolizes
the home to be built and shared by the couple. It is
open on all sides, just as Abraham and Sarah had
their tent open on all sides to welcome friends and
relatives in unconditional hospitality. The ceremony
was led by a favorite seminary professor/minister of
mine and a rabbi. Dick and I celebrate their choices
and have broken bread and shared the cup many

Friday nights before sundown. Once, on a sail down the Great Dismal Swamp that connects Virginia and North Carolina, we were all together: sons Scott and Greg, our daughters-in-law Freddi and Barbara, Dick and I. We docked in a small marina in North Carolina; it was Shabbat. We recited the blessings and observed with red wine and pizza for our bread to share. It was enough.

My son and daughter-in-law have given me the opportunity to learn more about and participate in Jewish traditions and rituals, which has helped prepare me for Jewish weddings. There is no rabbi in Cozumel, so I am often called on to officiate. Nuria and Ted chose Cozumel as the place they wanted to speak their marriage vows in a more traditional Jewish wedding. We heard the traditional Seven Blessings:

> You abound in Blessings, Adonai our God, who creates the fruit of the vine.

> You abound in Blessings, Adonai our God, you created all things for your glory.

> You abound in Blessings, Adonai our God, you created humanity.

You abound in Blessings, Adonai our
God. You made humankind in Your im-
age, after Your likeness, and You prepared for us a perpetual relationship.

May she who was barren rejoice when
her children are united in her midst in
joy. You abound in Blessings, Adonai
our God, who makes Zion rejoice with
her children.

You make these beloved companions
greatly rejoice even as You rejoiced in
Your creation in the Garden of Eden as
of old. You abound in Blessings, Adonai
our God, who makes the bridegroom
and bride to rejoice.

You abound in Blessings, Adonai our
God, who created joy and gladness,
bridegroom and bride, mirth and
exultation, pleasure and delight, love,
fellowship, peace, and friendship. Soon
may there be heard in the cities of
Judah and in the streets of Jerusalem,
the voice of joy and gladness, the voice
of the bridegroom and the voice of the

bride, the jubilant voice of bridegrooms from their canopies and of youths from their feasts of songs. You abound in Blessings, Adonai our God, You make the bridegroom rejoice with the bride.

No barefoot groom, Ted wore serious leather shoes as he prepared the glass to be broken. Because we were on the sand, he made a small platform, set the goblet carefully on it, and covered the goblet with a linen cloth. I said, "The ritual of breaking the glass is ancient in Jewish tradition. It dates back to the Talmud and has been celebrated throughout the world by Jews as a reminder that even as the Temple was destroyed so long ago in Jerusalem, there is still joy and future for God's people. In our times, the ritual is also a reminder of the suffering of Jews throughout history. It is certainly appropriate for us on this night in this place. Ted and Nuria, Mozel Tov!"

Our blessing was in the name of the God of Abraham and Sarah and our God today. The ceremony was followed immediately by a very non-Jewish mariachi band whose glorious music filled the night sky.

The Wedding Kiss

I want each couple to know that the wedding kiss is a part of the commitment; it is not just a romantic expression of happiness (although I hope it is that, too). The kiss is part of the ceremony because it is the first time sweethearts kiss as husband and wife. "Sealed with a kiss" is very real. I do not say those patronizing words, "You may now kiss the bride." It's entirely possible the bride wishes to kiss the groom! So in our preparation for the ceremony and when necessary, I simply say, "The wedding kiss." I never have to say it twice, but I almost always need to give a gentle reminder. Maybe it's just permission.

It is interesting for me to see the various ways couples wish to be introduced following the exchange of wedding vows. For couples from the Midwest in the United States, it is most often, "Mr. And Mrs. John Smith." Many women from other regions retain their family name so I introduce them as "John Smith and Mary Jones, husband and wife." Or, as with Sarah and Terry, the first names only. "Friends, please greet Terry and Sarah, husband and wife." I am guided by the wishes of the couple getting married. I give a "Cozumel Souvenir Certificate" to each couple, and it is a special moment when the bride signs the certificate for the first time, especially if she adopts her husband's surname. More than once, the bride has forgotten how to spell it!

Rizumi and Yasuyuki, a beautiful young Japanese couple, gave me my favorite wedding kiss story. They made the long trip from their homes in Osaka, Japan, to Cozumel for a beachfront wedding. We talked earlier about the trust a couple places in the wedding planner, the minister, all those who work together to make a beautiful and meaningful wedding ceremony. Now imagine a wedding couple getting married in a language as foreign as the island sand upon which they will stand for the ceremony.

With a great deal of trust and a little help from an interpreter, that's what Yasuyuki and Rizumi did. Neither spoke Spanish or English, though Rizumi could read some English. Before the wedding, with the interpreter's assistance, I slowly read over the ceremony to Yasuyuki and told him what he was promising; he smiled and nodded, but I could see that he was perplexed. I knew he would have even less help at the wedding since the interpreter would not be standing with us.

The date was February 14, the time was sunset. Rizumi wore a long white dress, carried a bouquet of white flowers, and her pearl jewelry was luminous. Yasuyuki, every inch the nervous groom, was dressed in a black tuxedo, his short black hair shining as brightly as his new patent-leather shoes. As his bride walked toward him, he smiled broadly and then he bowed a long, deep, respectful bow to Rizumi. She then bowed to him. Together, they faced me and they bowed again. I put my hands together and I bowed. A tradition so ancient, so lovely, so gentle. When I asked the groom, "Yasuyuki, do you choose Rizumi to be your wife?" he summoned up the exact right English words and said them loudly and clearly, "I will! I will!"

But I began this story to tell you about the wedding kiss; I have never been in the presence of such a beautiful tender kiss. I thought at that moment it was their first kiss. And perhaps it was.

Dorothy and her two best men. Dorothy's son, Kyle, stood in front with Brian as she began to walk down the aisle. Kyle, age 5, broke away and walked gravely toward his mom, offered her his arm, and escorted her to the waiting groom.

Troy had asked years earlier if I would officiate at his wedding when he "found the right woman." Cindy entered his life and Troy called with the news. I crossed the Yucatan Channel on the ferry for their special day on the Maya Riviera.

Framed by palms on the beach, Victoria and Michael exchange wedding vows that will change their lives forever.

Joel and Katie chose to hold their wedding in the Presbyterian Church on the island during his leave from active military duty. Katie is obviously thrilled as she takes Joel's hand to begin the ceremony.

Janine and Dallas recite their wedding promises. Many couples write their own vows that give personal meaning to traditional words of trust and fidelity.

Family and Friends and Why They Matter

Michael and Karen were very clear: they wanted the circle to symbolize their ceremony. Together with family and friends, they were 20 people standing under the bright morning sun, barefoot and forming a perfect circle. The bride and groom stood together with parents on either side. I began, "Circles are the perfect and most natural of shapes. The Sun is a circle. The Moon is a circle. Trees grow from circular trunks and flowers are most often a circle. The universe is a circle. Almost all shells from the sea around us are in the shape of a circle. Circles are perfect because they are without end. Karen and Michael, today you are surrounded by a circle of love."

The "circle of love" neither begins nor ends on the wedding day. In writing their own vows, many couples speak to each other as "best friend" or "soul mate." It is the constancy of that friendship that helps sustain many marriages in troubled times; to travel thousands of miles to share the wedding date with friends is no small feat. And to be asked to affirm God's blessing upon the bride and groom brings that deep friendship into sharp focus.

I often invite the bride and groom to "turn and look around you. You know who is here but just look! All these people who love and care for you enough to share this special day with you." I meet friends from the sandbox years, college roommates, even, on one occasion, a former spouse who made the journey to share in the wedding. At some weddings, years of silence and estrangement melt away in the warmth of what the ritual symbolizes.

Mikel and Clyde made elaborate and thoughtful plans months in advance of their summer wedding. A "scouting trip" helped them decide about flowers, the photographer, the rehearsal dinner, and wedding supper for more than 90 invited guests. Nothing was left to chance. You have seen Mikel and Clyde on the cover of this book; their wedding was a dream come true. The sky was heavy with rain clouds the morning of the wedding. Sunshine teased but by noon the decision had to be made: ceremony on the beach or in the hotel dining room. A dilemma. True to their dream, they elected to continue setting up the beach with flowers, chairs, and dining tables for all the guests. Each table centerpiece was a mix of sea treasures: pearls and shells. Candles flickered. The band played; Mikel and Clyde danced and sang. It was beautiful. Elegant. As the day turned to dusk, the sky filled with radiant colors of purple, red, gold. Just as they had planned. Their careful planning, gracious hospitality, and gratitude to family and friends were extraordinary. In the wedding program, they wrote, "We are truly grateful to our parents for their help in bringing us to this point in our lives. With their guidance, support, and example, we will begin our new life together. Thank you to all our family and friends for sharing in this memorable and joyful occasion. We also would like to remember our grandparents who could not be with us today, but are celebrating with us in spirit. Mikel and Clyde."

Being There

While I am talking about friends and family, let me say a word directly to you parents out there. If you are invited to your son's or daughter's wedding in a far-away place, and you are debating whether or not to buy that ticket and travel to that unknown place, do it! Your presence will bring such a special dimension to the wedding. And if you are the grandparent, take my advice and know that your grandchild will give you extra bonus points for the rest of your life.

It was a set of parents that made one ceremony particularly notable for me. A bride and groom wrote to ask if we could celebrate their wedding at sunrise. Because it was spring, the sun rose very early. On that day, I had to rise even earlier to drive across the island to the east shore in darkness. How I wished for a December morning! But there I was on that early morning, facing eight parents. Yes, eight; on the bride's side were her mother, father, stepmother, and stepfather and on the groom's side, the same grouping. Even more remarkable was the friendship they all shared and the seamless ease with which the bride and groom embraced all of their parents. Together, the parents helped to create a path of *luminaria* for the bride by placing short candles into the sand. As the sun rose over the beach, the bride walked down a candlelit path to meet her groom, who was dressed in officer dress whites. Despite my initial unspoken resistance, I've carried the picture of that morning with me ever since. When I asked the parents for their blessing, there was a chorus of "Yes, we do!" spoken with a unity I've often wished all parents would bring to their children's weddings.

No matter how much information I seek before preparing for a wedding, I am still often surprised. As I was just before a midday wedding in a lovely garden when I met six parents this time: the bride's mother and father and the groom's mother and stepfather and father and stepmother. But that was not the surprise. The surprise was that among the group, there were four religious affiliations: Jewish, Catholic, Protestant, and Buddhist. I hastily reviewed my prayers and blessings, thankful that they were fairly generic. I revised them to be inclusive of all the parents and reminded myself once again that it's a good thing that the weddings I have a part in are never one-size-fits-all. Because they don't. Weddings are meant to be as personal as the bride and groom standing before me, as personal as the families they come from. At the end of the ceremony, two of the parents told me they had been apprehensive that someone would be left out.

After I married one young couple, the groom's mother sent me this letter: "I am Bradd's mother and I want you to know you made their wedding so very special with your awesome message, warmth, and love. God blessed us ALL that day when he sent YOU to marry Bradd and Jada. You touched ALL our hearts!! When Bradd was in 8th grade, his ATV was hit by a pickup and we didn't know whether he would live, and if he did, we didn't know if he would be okay. He had a severe open head wound, concussion, contusions, cracked ribs, and a collapsed lung. Praise the Lord, God wasn't finished with him yet, and there hasn't been a day that goes by we aren't thankful for the gift of Bradd. We have always called him our 'miracle child.' When you almost lose your life or the life of someone close to you, it makes you appreciate the little things that are many times in this busy world taken for granted. Pastor Jean, I want you to know you were truly a blessing to us November 6th on Bradd and Jada's wedding day. We thought Cozumel was paradise and truly plan to visit again some day."

Dealing with Difficulty

As important as family and friends are to the couple getting married, they can also be obstacles to be overcome. We've all heard the stories and I've seen many family dramas being played out publicly and privately before, occasionally during, and after the wedding. When Cynthia and John got married, I played a starring role in the family drama, much to my dismay. Since most couples who come to Cozumel to get married are American or Canadian, the issue of the woman minister is generally a non-issue. Not always. Cynthia and John made extensive wedding plans by e-mail, and each letter was thoughtful and mature. I looked forward to being with them and was preparing to write their ceremony, incorporating the scriptures they chose. Then Cynthia wrote, "Jean, I am sure you have faced this before, but we have a problem with my parents. They are very conservative Baptists and they cannot accept a woman minister.

Please understand, this is not our wish, we really want you to marry us. However, it would be best if you could locate a man."

Cynthia and John were not children; both held responsible executive positions in the corporation where they worked. I pondered and then replied, "Cynthia and John, actually this has not been an issue in the past. For better or worse (no pun intended), I am the only English-language minister on the island. More important, however, is this: this is *your* wedding. What do *you* want?" They talked this over and decided the wedding we had planned was just what they wanted.

John and Cynthia arrived on the island two days prior to the wedding; we met to review the ceremony, conscious of parental disapproval. I suggested Cynthia's father might read one of the scriptures they had chosen, thereby making him feel more included. They thought that was a good idea, and we all thought we were settled.

Not so. The wedding day was beautiful with a shining sun and enough clouds to guarantee beautiful photos and a refreshing breeze blowing off the ocean. When Dick and I arrived at the hotel, we were directed to Cynthia and John's suite; outside, I saw a man walking very smartly across the garden. He was tall and slender, dressed in a dark suit, starched white shirt, and dark tie and wearing polished black shoes.

Not your ordinary garden walker. As he drew closer, I said, "You must be going to the wedding," to which he replied stiffly, "*I* am the father of the bride."

Extending my hand, I introduced myself as the minister and Dick as my husband.

Father of the bride said, "This is a Muslim wedding. Is that correct?"

"No, that is not my understanding..." I began.

He interrupted: "Well, Miss, if it is, I'll break your neck!"

Rarely at a loss for words, I was speechless. I walked away. Cynthia was waiting for me at her suite, greeting me with confidence and grace. I began, "I just met your father in the garden downstairs..." Before I could finish, she said, "That's why I want to talk with you. Will you please read all the scriptures?" Of course, I was happy to do so.

At the conclusion, her father and mother both spoke warmly about the ceremony. They explained they were Baptists but the church had "strayed too far" and they were looking for a more Calvinist church where they could serve as missionaries. Was there something here on Cozumel? It didn't take me a millisecond to say, "Actually, no."

Sometimes it is the mother of the bride whose expectations take my breath away. Many couples plan their paradise weddings from distances far from this tropical island—Minnesota, Canada, Spain, and beyond. And what makes the tropics so lush and beautiful? In part, the rain showers that can surprise us at any season of the year. It is the rain and the sun that make the flowers happy; it is the rain that makes brides and mothers of the brides so unhappy. One mother wrote to me, "Dear Minister: Please plan the wedding ceremony to begin just a few moments before the sun sets; I want my daughter's wedding kiss to be at the exact moment the sun drops below the horizon." I reminded her there are times the skies surprise; there is neither sun nor sunset. But I could promise her beautiful flowers.

In a Time of Joy and Sorrow

Couples often ask if I would include prayers of remembrance for friends or family members; sometimes they are especially poignant. Sharon and Tom planned their wedding for a year. The wedding party, more than 30 guests, was registered at a beautiful hotel. I met with the wedding couple Saturday morning when we selected Scripture readings for the Sunday afternoon ceremony. Sharon and Tom chose the passage from 1 John 4:7-12.

"Beloved, let us love one another, because love is from God; everyone who loves is born of God and knows God. Whoever does not love does not know God, for God is love. God's love was revealed among us in this way: God sent God's only Child into the world so that we might live through that Child. In this is love, not that we loved God but that God loved us...Beloved, since God loved us, so much we also ought to love one another."

At the conclusion of our planning, I left for home to write the ceremony. The entire wedding party chartered a boat for an afternoon of snorkeling and swimming. Sunday dawned sunny and perfect; the sky was blue, the water shimmered from the sun like a sea of diamonds. It was postcard perfect.

However, when I arrived for the ceremony, the hotel staff greeted me with shocking news: a favorite cousin of the bride had drowned on the snorkel excursion. He had a history of heart disease and his heart gave out. I went to the bride's room and learned that a decision had been made to continue the ceremony as her cousin would have wanted. I suggested we add another scripture reading in his memory and include him in our prayers of blessing.

We began: "Friends, we gather today to celebrate and bless the marriage of Sharon and Tom even as we grieve and give thanks for the life of our friend and cousin, James. The Bible offers us a beautiful poem in the Book of Ecclesiastes that wraps God's arms around us and reminds us that God's plan for life includes all experiences—in joy and in sorrow. That is God's promise."

Then the wedding ceremony continued as planned with a reading from the third chapter of Ecclesiastes, verses 1-8:

> For everything there is a season, and a time for
> every matter under heaven:
> A time to be born, and a time to die;
> A time to plant, and a time to pluck up what is
> planted;
> A time to kill, and a time to heal;
> A time to break down, and a time to build up;
> A time to weep, and a time to laugh;
> A time to mourn, and a time to dance;
> A time to cast away stones, and a time to gather
> stones together;
> A time to embrace, and a time to refrain from
> embracing;
> A time to seek, and a time to lose;
> A time to keep, and a time to cast away;
> A time to rend, and a time to sew;
> A time to keep silence, and a time to speak;
> A time to love, and a time to hate;
> A time for war, and a time for peace.

Despite the sadness of James' death, it was a celebration of life and hope.

In the Presence of Children

It is far more common in these past few years to have the children of one of the marrying couple or both at the wedding. Sometimes, they are not a visible part of the wedding. Todd and Dianne made Cozumel their vacation destination for many years. They are divers who established friendships with many Mexicans and Americans who shared their love for the dazzling beauty of our reefs and the sea life that inhabits them. It was natural that Dianne and Todd would choose this paradise to say their wedding vows. By the wedding day, Dianne was six months pregnant with their first child, who turned out to be a son, Ethan. They were thrilled. Dianne said to me, "Some people ask if we are getting married because I'm pregnant. But I tell them, 'I'm pregnant because we're getting married!'"

In the Church

Kent and Linda were two families uniting as one. They asked to celebrate their wedding in the church. On a beautiful day in June, the ceremony began at 4 o'clock. As we blessed the rings, Linda's 5-year-old daughter Teresa stood with her mother. After the bride and groom exchanged rings, they presented Teresa with a "family medallion," a silver disc worn on a chain. She asked me to bless her medallion and of course I did. Linda and Kent spoke words of commitment to her: to love and respect her as they grew together as one family. Kent and Linda were strong in their desire to include a Unity Candle as part of their wedding ceremony. I wrote this small piece for them:

"Candles are for giving. Candles give light in the darkness; candles give warmth in the cold. Candles give hope. From this common candle, Linda, Kent, and Teresa each lit their own candles—giving light and love and hope shared with one another. When one candle flickers and falters, it is rekindled by the light given by another's. Candles are for giving."

In one weekend mid-summer, I had four weddings: three with children. Children of the groom, children of the bride. Sons and daughters soon to become brothers and sisters. The trend continued into autumn. I tried to imagine the feelings of a child whose parents are standing with someone they (usually) know and care for, repeating strange words from a strange woman in a long purple robe. Many times Mom or Dad is tearful. It is understandably bewildering, sometimes frightening and uncomfortable. How is it possible such big changes in their lives can occur in just a few minutes? Surely there is a better way.

Within the week the opportunity presented itself. Jeff and Denise, Denise's son Josh and Jeff's daughter Leah all met with me two days before their wedding. All were in agreement I should create a special place in the wedding ceremony for the children. They were excited. Leah was ten, Josh almost six. I told them I would ask their parents to make promises to each other and I would ask them also. Grandparents and other relatives were among the guests.

Following the traditional exchange of vows between the bride and groom I asked the children to stand with me. I said, "Weddings are about making promises. But weddings are not just for the bride and groom, they are for you, too. These promises are called *vows* and are some of the most important promises your mother and dad will ever make in their lives. Now I want to ask you to make a promise.

"Leah and Josh, do you—each of you—promise to love and honor and share in the life of your new family?"

For her part Leah answered with a solemn and thoughtful "I will." Josh thought a bit and said, "I'll try."

And to the bride and groom: "Denise and Jeff, you are blessed this day not only by the vows you have spoken but also with a beautiful new son and daughter. Will you—each of you—promise to love and honor, respect and guide your children to become the people they are meant to be as you share life together as a family?"

Denise, touching Leah, and Jeff, touching Josh, looked into their eyes, and spoke a heartfelt "I promise."

Not for the First Time

Gail and Ben came to celebrate five years of a good marriage, leaving their three-year-old son home with grandparents. Gail was mid-way through chemotherapy and radiation therapy for cancer. I remember sitting across the desk from my own physician who spoke the words nobody wants to hear: "You have cancer." My own experience with cancer has given me insight and courage I otherwise would never have known.

Gail and Ben wanted a quiet private moment to recommit their love and their lives "for as much time as we have." Five of us stood together to mark this marriage: Gail, Ben, me, and a couple who made the trip with them. Barefoot, Gail was dressed in a summer peach-colored dress. When Ben appeared, he surprised Gail by wearing a shirt that matched her dress exactly. He presented Gail with a single white rose and knelt before her. He began, "Gail, we don't know what God has planned for us, but as long as we live I will love you and care for you." We asked God to bless their rings again and we read the passage from Ecclesiastes "For everything there is a season and a time for every matter under heaven..."

Later, walking on the beach, Gail said to me, "You know, I am terminal." I stopped, looked directly at her and said, "Gail, 'terminal' is where the bus goes. You are not terminal." She smiled and said, "Thank you for that. We'll be back next year!"

Is the glass half-full? Or half-empty? Do couples come to renew their wedding vows because they feel hope or something else? Each renewal carries its own story and the motivations of the couples who come are as unique as the couples themselves. Gail and Ben are good examples. They celebrated their solid foundation and their hope for a future life together.

Mary Jane and Eric also came to celebrate their past and what they hoped would be a bright future.

They came to Cozumel to celebrate a strong thirteen-year marriage. Accompanied by two young daughters who were the bridesmaids and a young son as the best man, theirs was a bittersweet celebration. Mary Jane had recently completed months of chemotherapy for an aggressive and growing cancer.

But the celebration was a gala. Eric made all the arrangements with extended families and more. While Mary Jane knew about the ceremony, she didn't know everything Eric had planned. And even I, with my resistance to surprises, was looking forward to seeing Eric's plans executed. Before the wedding began, I stood at the base of a circular stairway with the bridesmaids (ages 9 and 11) who carried small bouquets of cut flowers. In a loud voice I said, "It seems the bridesmaids are all ready. Shall we begin?" At this moment, three of Mary Jane's dearest friends slowly descended the stairs, one at a time. Each arrival brought hugs and tears. I explained to the children their mother was crying because she was happy, not sad. Finally, we were gathered, but my script contained one more cue: "Is there someone who would like to escort the bride?" At this point Mary Jane's two parents walked arm and arm down the same staircase. More hugs and tears. Then we began the simple ceremony that lifted the hearts of Mary Jane and Eric and those of everyone present. Myself included.

After a Divorce

Couples divorce for so many reasons, some they do not fully understand themselves. A good divorce can represent the same good faith reflection a good

marriage receives. For those who made their wedding
promises in the presence of God, the pain can be
compounded. Will God disapprove? Will God punish
me? Will the same God whose name was invoked
with love now abandon me? Or will this dependable
God hear the pain and remain steadfast even as
wedding promises were broken, trust lost, and hope
for reconciliation gone? The God I know doesn't leave
us hanging out to dry.

Statistics in the United States are not encouraging;
close to 50 percent of all marriages end in divorce.
Marriages do fail. And it can be an act of courage to
recognize that fact and end the marriage rather than
live an empty and sometimes damaging façade. Many
couples who are thinking about marrying again come
to the decision reluctantly if they have experienced
painful and hurtful earlier marriages. When people
have left such marriages, to renew this commitment
and re-speak the vows can be an act of courage as
much as an act of love. Their trust has been shattered
and they sense failure in themselves or their former
spouses. Perhaps both. Were their expectations too
high? Did they work at their marriage too little?
Were they not the people they believed they were?
Following earlier failed marriages, friends celebrating
their twenty-fifth wedding anniversary told me, "We
were two wounded birds who found each other."

Sometimes those wounded birds heal and find their way back to each other, which is what happened to Sandy and Jack. They married 21 years ago and knew it was forever. Friends since childhood, high school sweethearts, they married young surrounded by lifetime friends and relatives. Over the course of six years, they had three children: two girls and a boy. Sandy taught pre-school, and Jack managed an auto parts store. They worshipped together and ate Sunday dinner most weekends with their families. They took their children camping. In other words, they led middle-America lives, good folk.

Like others, though, over time, they grew apart, lived apart a while, finally agreed to an amicable divorce, including shared custody of their teenaged children.   Jack re-married, Sandy did not.   But their kids kept them in regular communication. As divorces go, theirs was civil, even thoughtful.

Jack's second marriage soon ended. He and Sandy began, little by little, to spend more time together, finally exploring the possibility of starting all over again. They set the date and chose Cozumel as the place to speak their "I Do's, Part Two."

Traveling with one other couple, Sandy and Jack met me on the beach at their hotel. We talked about new beginnings, about change, and opportunities for another chance; they were ready. We chose the passage from Ecclesiastes that I favor for second marriages; it suited the occasion perfectly. At sunset, the ceremony began. Jack arrived first, dressed in a silk print shirt and linen walking shorts. Sandy appeared in pressed cut-off jeans and an expensive white cotton over-sized shirt. Not exactly what most would call wedding attire.

I wondered if she took seriously—as Jack did—the vows they were preparing to speak. But when they did speak, when they exchanged new rings, when they bowed their heads for the final blessing, tears of happiness showed up on both of their faces. Sandy's first words: "I feel I am finally married. For the first time."

Music on the Beach

To be honest, I am partial to mid-life couples marrying for a second time; on a few occasions, for a third. Regardless of how they became single after an earlier marriage, they usually approach the wedding ceremony and the marriage itself with a deeper appreciation and greater commitment. Judith and Mario chose to celebrate their wedding with only one guest, Judith's daughter, Elizabeth, on the beach at an island hotel. Elizabeth, age 9, was a delight, happy, comfortable, and very "island" in her newly braided hair with flowers woven into a crown. The three made a beautiful family tableau as they stood in front of me. While Mario's son, Jascha, could not be with us, we included him in the prayers.

Music for a beach wedding is not an easy matter. For some, the sound of the waves is enough; for others, music is a necessity. Mario was one of those. He wanted to play a special CD he brought with him as background music while Judith walked across the sand to the altar. I explained the various limitations we faced but could see how disappointed he was. "Can you let me see the CD?" I asked. Perhaps I could bring the battery-operated cassette player we had at home to the beach. With just the family, it might work out. Mario returned from his room with a very special CD. The cover showed a photo of the classic temple and observatory from Chichen Itza, the Mayans' most renowned and revered ancient city. Under the title, "Piano Music for a Picture Album," the CD read, "All music composed, arranged, produced by Mario Ray." Of course, we would make it work! I took the CD home and Dick transferred the music to a tape. The cassette player provided very special musical accompaniment as Elizabeth walked toward me, followed by her smiling and gracious mother. At the end of the ceremony, the three walked arm in arm together to Mario's music.

I kept the CD.

The Wedding Garden

Terry and Sarah chose to arrive in Cozumel, their wedding destination, by cruise ship. They docked mid-morning with a party of 21 family members and friends. This was Terry's second wedding, Sarah's first. As high school sweethearts 15 years earlier, they had talked about marriage. Today, they would finally marry and the wedding carried their joy and hope. When I met with Terry to review the ceremony, he told me his first marriage was as a very young man. "This is forever," he said.

The wedding took place at Stephanie's beautiful wedding garden, lush with plants with sand sea and sky as our backdrop. Stephanie and Felipe fell in love and were married on the island of Cozumel. Soon Stephanie established and grew her own business as a wedding planner. Stephanie is the contact person for most weddings, both religious and civil, for hotels and many of the cruise lines. Three years ago she designed the wedding garden, a grassy space overlooking the sea.

As I stood at the altar with Sarah and Terry, I told them, aside from the microphone, "You have been to weddings before and you will go to weddings again. But this is your wedding and there will never be another just like it. It is my prayer that this ceremony makes your hearts glad." And the wedding began.

After a Death

When Dave and Connie began planning their Cozumel wedding, friends and family said "Not without us!" Result: 32 wedding guests arrived on a luxury cruise ship for a morning wedding on the beach. Anticipating the hot noonday sun, each guest received a pair of sunglasses in a variety of colors: green, orange, yellow, red. They were a colorful symphony in harmony with the flowers the bride and her daughters carried. Dave's 14-year-old son was his attendant.

Connie had been married for 20 years, living next door to her childhood home in the farmlands of Kansas. She was Mom to two teenage daughters when her world fell apart; her husband was killed in a highway accident. The thought of remarrying did not occur to her until three years later when Dave, a family friend and neighbor since childhood, made the thought seem like a good one. Dave had been married too but he and his wife had divorced years before. He was a single parent to his son, Sean, who had grown up with Connie's daughters. For Dave and Connie to say "I do" in paradise was a sweet moment, shared and celebrated by all.

They planned their wedding ceremony to include a poem, *On Your Wedding Day* by Nita Penfold, that spoke to them:

In a perfect world
I wish you a marriage
Like two mountains embracing,
Sharing the same foundation,
Lush growth intertwining wildly,
Seeds from each mountain
Germinated by the other.
In a perfect world, there would be no one
Needing to blast a tunnel between you
So that a road might run through.

In a perfect world, I would wish you a marriage
Like two sea currents, parallel, yet weaving
    through
One another, creating whirlpools in your wake;
By your very natures immutable, enhancing
One another and letting go, empowering
Each other to be free within your union.
In a perfect world, there would be no
Boulders to encircle, pulling you away,
    no sudden
Promontories to crash against in confusion.

But, we know, this is not a perfect world.
It has to be enough that you have found one
    another
To share your life's journey, enough
To cherish each other and day's end.

So I choose to wish for you that,
In this imperfect world, you will always have
    enough:
Both enough contentment and enough challenge
To hold you satisfied, enough strength to keep
    from
Clutching too hard so you never break the bond;
As solid as the mountains in endurance, growing
    together;
Enough peace to balance the heartache, the
    sorrows.

And I wish you such joy, playful,
Limitless like the sea, replenishing
As you wind your lives around one another's.
Love is the miracle that chose the two of you.
Remember, you two are the miracle
That will keep it always dancing.

Recommitment

Sometimes life gives us a refresher course in what we hold most dear. A threatening medical diagnosis. A job lost. A natural disaster such as the hurricanes this earthly paradise respects and dreads. The accident Bradd's mother wrote about. Other times, the reminder is a happy one: the birth of a child, a friendship restored, a random act of kindness that gladdens the heart. Certainly, a wedding anniversary offers such a moment: time to revisit and express the love that blossomed into marriage at an earlier time. Whether at one year, 50, or more, an anniversary can be time for reflection and recommitment by both husband and wife. A ceremony to renew wedding vows is not always the way of recommitment but it is one way to put feelings of love into ritual.

When Gary and Laurie first saw the movie *Against All Odds* in 1984, they could not imagine how it would become a part of their lives. The movie was filmed at the ancient Mayan sites Tulum, Chichen Itza, and on the beach at Playa Palancar on Cozumel Island. Both were captivated by its serenity and beauty. "Please take me there" Laurie said to her husband. And so they visited many times, always returning to the beautiful Playa Palancar, which Laurie found romantic, on the south end of the island. It was only natural they decided to choose Playa Palancar to renew their wedding vows on the occasion of their twenty-fifth anniversary. Their friend and pastor Dale Pratt, who could not be with us, wrote his wishes for them and provided a copy suitable for framing as an anniversary gift.

On an overcast day marked by a gentle spring rain, Laurie and Gary renewed their wedding vows and exchanged rings. Their pastor's greeting read:

To Gary and Laurie as you celebrate your Twenty-Fifth Wedding Anniversary:

"Love endures all things. Love never fails" (1 Corinthians 13: 7, 8)

The word "endure" can carry with it just a hint of foreboding...a feeling that I'll be called on to tolerate situations or emotions that are uncomfortable or disconcerting to me...I'll be thrown into difficult circumstances and be expected to, well, to endure.

Perhaps no single word could more adequately describe long love than: Endure. And to remain with love, and the one we share that deep, refreshing well with for 25 years is a testament to endurance.

No love comes without struggle, and no one walks away from the testing times a victor unless they hang onto their love longer than the pain inflicted in the tests of strength... which will endure?...the pain or the love?

It is obvious to me that to you, my friends, love is stronger...has endured and will endure. It gives me great pleasure to congratulate you on your 25 years of marriage, and it gives me even greater satisfaction to applaud your endurance. May faith and hope continue to nourish your love, giving it strength for yet another...day? Test? Year? Vacation? Margarita? Decade? Moment?

Enjoy this moment...of celebration—
everything your love has been and all it can
be! And give it room to: Endure...one more
moment, one more test, one more pleasure.

My love to you and for you.

—used with permission

Wow!

"Wow!" is the best word to describe Sam and Teri's
tenth wedding anniversary. They came to Cozumel on
their first-ever vacation in those 10 years of marriage.
Teri's sister and her husband and Sam's brother and
his wife came with them. Born and raised in a small
town in west Texas, Sam and Teri had not traveled
more than 50 miles from home. Now, finally, this
milestone anniversary trip. Their corner of Texas is
far from the sea so neither had ever seen it. Sam and
Teri arrived on a cruise ship; it goes without saying,
they had never seen a cruise ship before. They were
captivated by everything: the tall stately palm trees,
the wide white stretches of beach. "Wow!" was Sam's
frequent expression of unrestrained delight.

Now imagine this: on the day of celebration, Sam
and Teri were both 26 years old. They married at
sixteen, and had two children, ages 5 and 7. But the
vacation was for Mom and Dad. They asked me to
prepare a simple ceremony to renew their wedding
vows and bless their rings. And they asked one thing

more: May the sister and brother each speak? Of course.

First Teri's sister spoke, then Sam's brother. Each read letters of love and blessing from their parents, blessings they could not offer to the young teenagers determined to marry and make a life for themselves 10 years earlier. The letters were beautiful and made the family circle complete. Wow!

"When I Am 64"

Mary and Chuck are another of my favorite couples. Truthfully, I find something special in the stories of all the couples I work with on wedding or recommitment ceremonies. Mary and Chuck came to Cozumel to celebrate 25 years of marriage and commit themselves to a shared future. Twenty-five more. Or more. They arrived by cruise ship on a very warm last day in May in the company of their three adult children, a newly announced fiancé, and Chuck's parents whose marriage has thrived for 58 years. They came to renew wedding vows spoken long ago at their wedding held in Mary's family home, to speak personal words of recommitment, to bless and renew original wedding rings, and yes, to dance. This is what they came to Cozumel to say and to do. And they did it all.

The celebration began aboard ship with a presentation of t-shirts created by their daughter

Ashley. Printed on the front were the words, "Anniversary Cruise 2004 Chuck and Mary 25 Years." On the back was, "When I am 64," the title of the song by the Beatles Mary and Chuck had played at their wedding. When Mary and Chuck arrived at the beach where the renewal ceremony would be held, their children gave them engraved silver goblets. Each complete by itself, together they formed a single work in the shape of a heart. Upon one was written, "Immature Love: I love you because I need you." Upon the other, "Mature Love: I need you because I love you." (Eric Fromm)

Our earlier correspondence guided me in preparing the ceremony. "We would like a non-religious ceremony where the focus is on our past, current, and future commitment to each other and to our family. We will be bringing a CD of special music we have mixed ourselves." I chose to read from Kahlil Gibran's reflections on marriage. And it was a wise choice, a long-time favorite of Chuck's and, until this day, not known to Mary.

The small ceremony was on the beach on a windy afternoon. A large umbrella materialized to provide shade for us from near-summer heat. Son Andrew carried the rings in a small scallop shell. Mary and Chuck chose to dance together between the recommitment of their rings and the blessing. Each spoke these words: "Mary (Chuck), I place this ring on your hand again, as a sign of my continued love and fidelity. That with all that I have, and all that I am, I honor you. And I will love you forever." Then the music, "When I am 64," of course. On soft sand, they danced together. Then Mary danced with Chuck's father, then with son Andrew while Chuck danced with each of his daughters and his mother. As the music gradually faded, we formed a full circle that included all the family; the newly engaged son-in-law-to be; Dick, my husband; Cecilia, the wonderful wedding coordinator; and me. We held hands and prayed. There was enough joy and enough blessing to go around and plenty left over for a rainy day.

A Rainy Day Story

I want you to know about another very special couple, Kathy and John, who arrived by cruise ship with their three teenagers in the summer of 1999. Kathy and John were married eight years earlier, a second marriage for each. Kathy came to the marriage with a son who was eight at the time, John with two daughters a bit younger. Both Kathy and John are public school teachers in the Midwest; they are by no means affluent.

Three years into their marriage, Kathy fell and the blow to her head wiped out her memory; she had classic amnesia. She could not remember her name, her children's names, or her husband's name. She lost her life story. Over time, most of the memories resurfaced, and Kathy returned to the classroom. The one missing piece was their wedding. Her doctors were certain that the memory was gone forever.

Kathy suggested to John that perhaps they might have another wedding, this time in Cozumel, to replace the missing memory. John went to work on the Internet, locating a wedding planner on the island. They corresponded, but the price was too high. Kathy said it had been a good idea, but no thank you.

Then came the next letter from John: "In the future, please write to me at my office, not at home." I am wary of one part of a twosome making plans for both. When the wedding coordinator called me and told me what Kathy and John had been planning, I thought it was a beautiful idea. Until I learned that John was continuing plans that Kathy had given up on. The wedding planner relayed my reluctance to John, who agreed to share his plan with the whole family before leaving home. Next step: a shopping trip to the mall to outfit all three kids; new dresses for the girls and slacks and a white shirt for Kathy's son.

Everybody was ready.

The family arrived by horse-drawn carriage at the hotel where the ceremony would take place on a small

pier on the beach. Kathy's son, now a tall young man
of 16, and John's daughters, ages 12 and 13, came
into the hotel first, followed by their parents. Kathy
carried a large bouquet of white flowers tied with
colorful ribbons. She immediately turned to me, "I
am a shy person. Will there be lots of people around
us?" I assured her that while we were on the hotel's
open beach, we would be apart and nobody would
interfere or crowd us. We walked together through
the hotel lobby, across the swimming pool deck, and
around the outside restaurant to a small platform
overlooking the sea. The ceremony began with my
words:

> Kathleen and John, you have been here
> before. Not in this geographic space, but in the
> same spaces of your hearts. You came together
> eight years ago, took one another's hands, and
> made promises to one another in the presence
> of God.

> You promised to love. To cherish. In good
> times and in bad. You were younger then
> and your love for one another was fresh and
> mysterious. You were the same people then
> that you are today, but less so. Years have
> brought wisdom, a deeper understanding of
> what love is all about. You have known tragedy
> and you have known hope and together you

have shared triumph. Only with time together, loving and caring for one another, by the grace of God can we learn who we truly are.

Today, you come together again; to take one another's hands and renew your promises to one another in the presence of God and your children, Amanda, Melissa, and Josh. The promises you make do not guarantee a happy or perfect marriage, it is commitment they represent. That commitment seeks to honor the choices and support the beliefs each of you carries, to treat with tenderness and caring the inner person you have chosen to be with. Each of you has found your soul mate.

Only when you have reached deep inside into the heart and mind of yourself and one another...only then can you truly say, "I love you for now and until eternity."'

The Apostle Paul wrote words familiar but so appropriate for this day: (Reading from 1 Corinthians 13, which is reprinted on page 109-110.)

Kathleen and John, are you prepared, with God's help, to speak your promises again? Please repeat after me:

I, John, celebrate you, Kathleen, as my wife. To have and to hold from this day forward...

For better or worse, for richer, for poorer, in sickness and in health...

As Kathy said those words back to John, she wrapped her arms around her husband and held him close; my throat filled with a lump that made it difficult to swallow. I felt I was intruding in their most private moment, and it remains forever in my memory as one of the truly perfect weddings. We continued with the wedding vows, blessed their rings, and prayed our closing blessing. A crowd from the hotel had gathered at the restaurant above us to whistle and cheer the wedding kiss. And shy Kathy turned to them, waving her bouquet and wearing an unforgettable smile. As we said our goodbyes, Josh said to me, "Thank you. You have made my mom very happy."

In War and Peace

"In war and peace" are not part of the vows that couples make when they marry but perhaps it should be. Since September 11, 2001, the ground has shifted for thousands of women and men, husbands and wives, mothers and fathers, who were called to active duty in Afghanistan and Iraq. Their dreams are deferred, if not abandoned; their futures are shifted, if not shattered. And these same hopeful, trusting, loving couples are beginning to pick up broken dreams and often broken promises as they return to the civilian lives they once knew. Men and women cannot experience war up close and personal, awaken to the rattle of automatic weapons and the shrill whistle of missiles, witness the deaths of combatants young enough to be in school and non-combatants just like the kids they left at home, and not be forever changed. Those who have engaged in war must find a way back from the horrors of combat to the lives they left behind, the husbands and wives and children left behind.

Men and women return to their homes strangers. They are no longer the husband/father/brother/son that left. They are no longer the mother/wife/sister/daughter that left. Some have witnessed and participated in monstrous acts they wish to bury forever in the sands of memory. Anger. Drugs, legal and illegal. Too much power. Too little power. Shattering pain that doesn't quit. Once healthy bodies now twisted and broken. Jobs transferred and work lost forever.

What does "in sickness and in health" really mean? How can we bring meaning to the words so smoothly spoken, "in joy and in sorrow"? This is a compelling challenge to ministry and to faith itself.

In my experience with couples rebuilding lives together, there is a healing that I believe can be part of recovery: recovery of hopes and dreams, recovery of the person's heart and soul. This is the ritual of renewing wedding vows. This can mark the new beginning, the re-entry into a marriage with wholeness and hope. The ceremony can be simple. I invite couples to choose a scripture that has meaning for them; for some, it is the scripture read at their wedding. For some, the wedding was a military declaration spoken in haste and remembered only for what it lacked. In a sense, the renewal of their vows is their *first* wedding.

Still others have lived a lifetime in a year or two. They are in a new place in their lives and the presence of God has transformed their faith; some more, some less. But very few are not changed in their beliefs in some way.

Of course, the passage from 1 Corinthians 13:1-8 is appropriate. Sherri and Cliff, whose life as a family was turned upside down by the war, came to renew their vows in hopes it would give them a chance to start all over again. I suggested the Corinthians text. When Sherri heard the end of the passage, "...Love bears all things, believes all things, hopes all things, endures all things. Love never ends," she rejected it. Adamantly. "'Love never ends' just isn't true. Love does end. That's what we're trying to do: make it begin again. Please, let's read something else." So we did. They, and many couples, chose the poem from

Ecclesiastes 3: "For everything there is a season and a time for every matter under heaven....a time for war and a time for peace."

Many couples, though not all, can recapture what war has taken from them. I believe we must stand with them, bear all things with them, believe all things with them, hope all things with them, endure all things with them. That's what Paul says love is about. It's what I believe ministry is all about.

Decisions, Decisions, Decisions

When a couple says to me, "We've decided to get married" it sounds as though once "The Decision" has been made, just a little fine-tuning may remain. End of story. But, ah, not so fast. That first decision is but the beginning of many. I don't mean just the color of the nut cups and napkins, but the serious decisions that follow— the life decisions. Brides and grooms will make different decisions, choose various options, but even in the most challenging situations the mutual agreement leads to a more harmonious future.

Overcoming Obstacles

Coming to a decision to marry may seem easy. "All you need is love," right? Those famous songwriters may have thought so but the truth is marriage takes a lot of work. Some of that hard work takes place before the ceremony and that is a good thing. I came to know Chris and Debbie before I ever laid eyes on them through a series of letters they each wrote to me, working out an issue that was coming between them and the wedding they longed for. They allowed me to share some of our correspondence with you.

First, a letter from Chris:

Dear Jean,

I want you to know how much I appreciate your generous and warm offer of allowing us to celebrate our wedding at your home. Thank you so much! We are both excited and looking forward to meeting you. I am sure it will be everything we have dreamed of and more; things just have a way of working out like that. It's amazing. We went back and forth so many times about how we want to do this, and things are just falling into place perfectly. We would definitely like you to prepare a prayer for the wedding and any scripture readings you feel would be appropriate and meaningful to us. One other thing I would like if possible: some sort of candle-lighting ceremony similar to what a couple would do in a Catholic wedding where the bride and groom light a candle together from the liturgical candle. I would like to include my daughter in that, to signify our union as a family and our commitment before God. That is important to me, as our marriage is not legally recognized. The only people attending the wedding will be Debbie, me, my 16-year-old daughter, and her friend who is joining us on our holiday.

Debbie is Unitarian; I am Catholic. We have slightly different beliefs about religion, God, and prayer. We discussed this tonight, and she feels okay with a prayer and scripture read at the ceremony as well as [the outline we are providing]. Thank you for your assistance; please write with any questions. Chris

Chris writes again: "What do you do when one of the two people who are about to get married suddenly realizes that, hey, that Unitarian I met three years ago really ISN'T going to become Christian and now isn't sure about wanting to have children?"

Debbie wrote:

Chris and I have been together for three years. Since getting your message yesterday, Chris was interested that you are member of the United Church of Christ and did some reading. Maybe it could become "our" church. I thought that the UCC sounded nice but since I was 15 (I am 33 now), I believed that Christ was not the only teacher. A few years ago, I went on a spiritual journey and attended several churches and realized that the Christian ones didn't feel right for me. I don't believe that

Christ is the one and only teacher, and I am
not into worship. To me, true spiritual leaders
need love, not worship.

Chris is a Mormon-turned-Catholic and
suddenly is extremely angry with me and has
asked me more pointed questions than ever
about my spirituality and the answers I give
seem wrong every time. It is not a question of
loving me, not wanting to marry me, but until
last night a child or two was very much in the
plan. Chris doesn't feel we can have children
unless we both practice a Christian religion
and both participate. I don't have the desire to
convert, and we really differ on how we would
raise a child. Chris would want them to be
the same religion, and I would want to expose
them to lots of things. That seems worrisome...
I wonder how much of this is just normal pre-
wedding stress, trying to get the big issues out
of the way. Or is scared and trying to push me
away a bit.

I know this is more than you asked for, but
the UU minister is out of town. I'd call a priest
(I thought it might be a good idea if we spoke
with one together), but I don't know any. I may
yet make an appointment. You are the closest
thing we have to a spiritual guide at this
moment. Lastly, if you feel comfortable, (I'm

making a big assumption that you will even have time to respond), responding to me only would be best. Chris doesn't turn to others during times like this; I do. However, if you don't feel comfortable doing that, please just let me know. I would understand and still be very grateful to have you perform our ceremony. It means the world to me.

Warmest Regards, Debbie

My response was long—theological in part:

Debbie, Dear Debbie,

How I wish you and Chris were here for a conversation rather than you having to trust a stranger over cyberspace. Thank you for trusting me with your difficult questions. I wish more couples would explore these significant issues of faith before they wed. I will try to respond as though we were speaking together; perhaps some wisps of clarity will emerge. First, theologically I have to agree with you; I, too, believe Christ was a great teacher. I disagree about worship: I believe we need the community of believers in order to express faith and offer support to one another. However varied that may be. I am not high on doctrine, but I do care deeply about ritual and I think that is better expressed in worship than on the golf course or looking at a mountain.

It is a leap for anyone to make—from Mormon to Catholic. Both are hierarchical and extremely structured. So I can understand why the Unitarian tradition is bewildering. I cannot imagine a priest would be helpful, both because the Catholic Church does not respect same-gender couples and because the only marriages recognized by the church are those between Catholics married by priests in the church. The church does expect every child born to a Catholic parent to be raised Catholic.

I hope this helps and does not complicate your decisions; you both have set upon a journey worthy of your finest sense of integrity. Your questions are too important to dismiss and your potential for growth together is life-giving. I will respect whatever decision you make.

Faithfully yours, Jean

Chris wrote again:

Dear Jean,

Debbie told me about the letter she sent to you and your thoughtful response today. You have been so thoughtful and supportive; I never dreamed we would have a minister performing our wedding ceremony who would be this way.

I want to give you some background on how I feel as well.

I was raised Mormon, as my mother was. My father is not religious. I was basically sent to church alone (to this church that stresses the importance of family and is so family-oriented). I often went with neighbors. My siblings refused to go; my mother did not live by the church teachings or attend. After taking Mormon seminary classes in high school, I realized I really did not believe in the whole Mormon thing. I also did not feel part of the community of the church. Somehow, I didn't fit and I felt I was on the outside looking in. I attended several churches and ended up attending a Catholic church regularly. I must say, I was attracted by the Catholic Church community and the rituals more than anything. Something about them helped me feel at home, warm and comfortable and connected to God through the ritual and the community. I believe God is in the church community more than anything; it isn't just the priest representing God.

I always wanted and dreamed of having a family, going to church together, sharing it at whatever level felt good. Sort of like the white picket fence dream. It hurts to think of me and future children going off to church, incomplete without Debbie, having her absent in that ritual. I would probably rather not go than feel that way. I believe church is so important for children, that it teaches them so much, and I wish we were united in this.

I guess we could just not go, like we are now, but I would feel guilty not providing my children with that. This probably isn't making sense to you; it really isn't to me. I was hoping for clarity, sometimes writing helps. Sorry about the rambling.

I know I do not want to put off our marriage. I love Debbie more than anything, and I think we can work this out in time. I can't imagine my life without her. We love each other enough to find a common ground. Thanks for listening. Sincerely, Chris

I don't know what their process was as they worked on their divisions. What I do know is that we gathered together for their wedding on a sunny December morning in the garden of my home. Chris and Debbie both wore long white gowns. We read this passage from the Book of Ruth:

Entreat me not to leave thee, or return from
    following after thee.
For whither thou goest, I will go, and whither
    thou lodgest, I will lodge;

And thy people will be my people, and thy God
   my God.
Where thou diest, I will die, and there I will be
   buried.
The Lord do so to me and more also
If aught but death part thee and me.

A Step Before Marriage

On a few occasions I have been asked to help
create a commitment ceremony, something short of
a wedding that may come later. I do so with great
caution for fear that those standing before me will be
content to "play at getting married" without taking
the commitment seriously. But for some, it has been
the beginning of healing. Larry and Lois came for
such a ceremony. Each had emerged from difficult,
even dangerous, marriages to find each other. The
idea of marriage was overwhelming, but they wanted
to ritualize their love with the blessing of God in the
presence of Larry's brother. We chose a small beach
where Lois and Larry promised to grow in love for and
trust in one another. "Always I will be honest with
you," they each said to the other. At the conclusion
of the ceremony, Larry asked me to read a portion of
a prayer often attributed to the Navajo:

Now you will feel no rain, for each of you will be
   shelter to the other.

Now you will feel no cold, for each of you will be
     warmth to the other.
Now there is no loneliness for you, now there is
     no more loneliness.
Now you are two bodies, but there is only one
     life before you.
Go now to your dwelling place, to enter into your
     days together.

With tears in their eyes, the two brothers told
me, "This prayer is in memory of our mother. We are
Navajo people; our mother is with us today."

Surprises Seldom Work

I need to insert a word of caution into this chapter
and tell those of you planning a ceremony what *not* to
do when planning a recommitment ceremony. When
I urged John to share his wedding plans with Kathy
before they arrived, I did not realize how prophetic
I had been. Now I am older and wiser. I do not like
surprises, at least not where wedding anniversaries
are concerned. I believe that a couple sharing a
marriage should plan the anniversary event together.
One hand clapping is how I view either husband or
wife making surprise plans for the spouse. This story
may persuade some of you out there who think your
spouse would love a surprise:

Carol and Tom* had been married 25 years. They
came to our island paradise to renew their wedding

vows. The ceremony included their young adult daughters and the gift of a beautiful new ring. A *real* celebration. Right? Wrong. Tom had not included Carol in any of the elaborate planning, which included a white linen suit for Tom and a taxi to drive them to a special restaurant overlooking the sea. Tom and their daughters exchanged knowing smiles, but Carol was the guest. The outsider.

I met them with words of congratulations and could see she was bewildered. In fact, she was humiliated. "Who else knows about this?" she demanded to know. It only got worse. "Aunt Margaret and the neighbors, Grandma..." One daughter began. A whole truckload of work colleagues. Everybody but Carol. She was not amused. And poor Tom didn't have a clue. When some measure of calm was restored and Tom presented her with a dazzling ring, she could only say, "I didn't know. I don't have anything for you. I wish you had told me."

Like Carol, I had not been told about the surprise. As I watched and heard her reaction, I vowed to never let that happen again. Alas, it did. A similar action and reaction. A proud well-meaning husband, an embarrassed unhappy wife. The surprise element caught me by surprise. Now my policy is set: no surprises. Within the event itself, surprises can be beautiful, tender, and deeply meaningful. The event itself, however, is like a good chateaubriand, created to be shared.

Fresh from this experience, I was contacted by a representative from a large hotel asking me to officiate at a tenth anniversary renewal of wedding vows. Wiser now, I asked who was making the request and what the person could tell me about the couple. "It's a surprise," Ms. Hotel began. Bells went off in my head. "The wife wants to surprise her husband with a beautiful ceremony and dinner for just the two of them. Will you do it?"

"No," I replied, "and this is what I hope you will do: Ask the wife who is planning this surprise to share her plans with her husband; it's only fair. Experience has taught me that such an occasion must be mutually agreeable. If it is, I will be happy to officiate at a renewal ceremony." Fortunately, she did call. Result? The husband's immediate response was "Absolutely not! I've been through that once and that's enough." Maybe some pastoral counseling would have been a better option.

Conclusion

Many couples return to Cozumel to celebrate an anniversary. One day I was standing on the beach with my back to the sea, preparing to begin the wedding ceremony, when a man attired in full snorkel mask called to me from the surf. "Hi! It's me! You married my wife and me last year."

I welcome letters or return visits that fill in the years since the bride and groom said "I do" in paradise.

Alayna and Cleve made the long trip from their home in Alberta, Canada, to speak their wedding vows in paradise. Accompanied by parents and friends, the elegant gracious couple chose a beautiful hotel beach for the ceremony. I was prepared: my purple robe was pressed; the stole I chose was hand-woven in Guatemala. Nothing shabby about this wedding party. Suddenly the groom's mother exclaimed, "Oh, Jean! You have lost your earring." I looked down to the tile walkway—fortunately, we were not on the sand—and there at my feet was the fallen earring, a favorite silver earring with an amethyst stone. The back to hold it in place had fallen earlier. We retrieved the earring but I had no back piece until Cleve said, "Here, take mine. I promised I would take out my earring for the ceremony and just forgot." So with the groom's help, I completed my "grooming" and the wedding began.

Five years later, Alayna wrote to say they were returning to Cozumel to celebrate their anniversary. They renewed their vows and recommitted their love and their future together. It is not my custom to present the wedding couple with a personal gift, however, for Cleve, I made an exception and presented him with a jewelry box containing one small silver earring back. Just for a future emergency.

When I stand before so many beautiful young—and not so young—couples, I think beyond the joy of the wedding day and I wonder if they do too. I think about the future they have committed to together, the promises they speak. The promises are so grand and hopes are so high. Some are marrying for the first time and others speak wedding vows for the second or even third time trusting that "this time it will be better."

"To love and to comfort...in sickness and in health...in joy and in sorrow...in plenty and in want."

Thoughts of love, health, joy, and plenty come easily. Then I think about the stress of life in not such good times. I think about the stress on couples facing life with mental and physical challenges—their own or those they love—or the death of loved friends and family. The joy and stress that a first-born or chosen child brings to a married couple. What I want for the couples I marry and for every couple making this sacred commitment is that they are a comfort to each other in times of sorrow and hardship and a joy to each other in times of happiness and celebration.

Christine and Christopher were married in a ceremony filled with their loving families and 25 friends who made the trip from Massachusetts to share the special day. Chris, the bride, used her nickname "Bean" to avoid confusion with Chris, the groom. Chris was a handsome healthy-looking young man whose eyes glowed with unabashed adoration for his "Bean" and she responded in kind. Theirs was a bittersweet wedding; Chris was a cancer survivor who had just been diagnosed with recurring cancer. But they were committed to one another and to his full recovery. When they spoke the words "...in sickness and in health..." their voices rang with heartfelt meaning. I pray for them and a long life together. In the course of several visits to Russia, I learned to sing "God grant you many years" in place of "Happy Birthday." That is my prayer for Chris and Bean.

In the spring of 2003, a couple from Chicago asked for a ceremony to bless the husband's wedding ring on the occasion of their first anniversary. In the tenth month of their first year of marriage, he lost his ring and truly dreaded telling his wife. When he delivered his carefully chosen words of confession, her response was quick and clever: "Well, let's go to Mexico on a cruise! We'll pick out a new ring and certainly somebody can help us." I was the fortunate somebody who created a short ceremony for them. Arriving with one daughter, age 16, and her best friend, the group came directly to our home and we celebrated on the beach beneath our favorite sea-grape tree, an old, twisted, sturdy shade tree where we were serenaded by a delightful trio of singers with their instruments. One played a traditional folk guitar while another thumped a large guitar-like string instrument, and the third plucked on a hollow box with metal keys called a marimbol. Their music was a joy to hear. At the conclusion, the groom observed they had been married for just a year, he had two wedding rings, and a trip to Mexico; not bad. Not bad at all.

And they danced together on the sand. Which is a good way to think of the life that follows a wedding or recommitment ritual. Even better than "happily ever after" because a dance is never perfect and reaching its perfect moments takes practice, missteps, maybe even a few tumbles.

Epilogue
November, 2005

The island of Cozumel, our paradise, receives close to two million visitors each year; they come by air, land, and sea. And they are warmly welcomed. We *need* them; tourism is the basis of the island's economy. However, at the end of October, 2005, Hurricane Wilma arrived uninvited and definitely unwelcome. It was Mexico's "perfect storm." The largest hurricane on record, it was huge and slow. Oh, so slow. Water in the Gulf of Mexico was uncommonly hot; the hurricane gained strength and then struck the region with its greatest impact on Cozumel. For more than 60 hours, Wilma just hung around and hovered. She dumped more than 5 feet of rain and packed winds over 150 mph. Though it was designated a Category 5 storm, the highest possible rating, I was convinced it broke the scale at Category 10. The damage was catastrophic, not a word I employ lightly.

The hurricane was expected to land Thursday, October 20. Hotels were evacuating all guests and weekend weddings were advanced to that Thursday. I changed my schedule to officiate at two weddings that afternoon, one at three o'clock and one at five. By luck, they were to be at the same hotel. Dick and I arrived as rain fell off and on from darkening skies. As we approached the wedding site, hotel guests rushing to take the option to leave immediately on a six o'clock charter flight passed us by. The bride and groom for the later wedding were among the crowd. The bride carried her bouquet as she dodged the raindrops. We delayed the three o'clock wedding for over a half hour and finally moved under shelter from the rain. The ceremony was not smooth, but everyone agreed it was memorable. Then the sun came out.

Aftermath

All hotels here were closed for months. The popular wedding garden on the south end of the island is bare of all the trees and flowers that gave it such beauty. But we're in the tropics; they will reassert themselves. Weddings, of course, were postponed or cancelled for weeks or months. Brides and grooms arriving by cruise ship had the option of having their Cozumel weddings aboard ship.

But the qualities that make this island so beautiful, the people that make this island so lovely will survive. We were not Paradise Lost, we were just Paradise Missing for a while.

Appendix One: Ceremonies

Let's look at some wedding ceremonies. Most couples want a traditional ceremony and although each ceremony is similar, each is uniquely written for the bride and groom.

Weddings

Terry and Sarah

Terry and Sarah arrived on Cozumel by cruise ship in the company of 21 friends and family members. The ceremony was in the wedding garden facing the sea.

Minister: Dear friends, we are gathered together in the sight of God to witness and bless and celebrate the joining together of Sarah and Terry in holy marriage. We come to surround them with our prayers and to share in their joy.

Weddings are one of life's most precious rituals; they bind us to the past with the memories of love, and offer the promise of a future shared together in love. Every wedding is a holy and sacred moment. We do not need to be in a church or house of worship to ask God's blessing. God is present with us here and now.

Sarah and Terry, you have chosen this place of special beauty to begin your life together as a family. Your families and friends stand with you on this wonderful day. You are surrounded by the sounds and sights of the sea. Such beauty is universal; your union with one another is universal and eternal.

To the parents: The marriage of Sarah and Terry creates a new family just as it unites your own. Do you parents here present ask God's blessing upon Terry and Sarah as they make their solemn wedding promises?

Parents: We do.

Minister: To the family and guests: You have been invited and you have traveled a long distance to share in this wonderful day. You are more than witnesses, you are participants in this grand event! Terry and Sarah marry this day in the midst of the affection and friendship each of you brings; your presence here is your greatest gift to them and they thank you for being with us. The good wishes of family and friends will strengthen this new family and is a source of special joy. Will you, as family and friends, offer your support and ask God's blessing upon Sarah and Terry as they prepare to begin their married life together?

Family and friends: We will.

Minister: Sarah and Terry, I ask you now, in the presence of God, your friends, and your families, to declare your intention to enter into union with one another.

Terry, do you choose Sarah to be your wife, to live together in holy marriage? Will you love her, comfort her, honor and keep her in plenty and in want.... in joy and in sorrow...in sickness and in health, and forsaking all others, be faithful to her so long as you both shall live? [Notice I have selected the word "choose" rather than take; there is something possessive about "take" that seems harsh. Choose, by contrast, feels inviting. And I am sure most of us would rather be chosen than taken.]

Terry: I do.

Minister: Sarah, do you choose Terry to be your husband, to live together in holy marriage? Will you love him, comfort him, honor and keep him in plenty and in want...in joy and in sorrow...in sickness and

in health, and forsaking all others, be faithful to him
so long as you both shall live?

Sarah: I do.

Minister: Please pray with me. To the God that
is holy and makes us whole: We give thanks for
the lives of Sarah and Terry. We ask your blessing
upon their holy union. We pray that the love here
expressed for one another will continue to grow and
deepen. We give thanks for the families and friends
who have nurtured their lives. You create love that
unites us into the human family. We praise you for
your presence with us, and especially with Terry and
Sarah, as they make their solemn marriage promises.
Amen.

The Exchange of Vows
Terry: I, Terry, choose you, Sarah, to be my wife,
to have and to hold...from this day forward, for better
or worse...for richer, for poorer, in joy and in sorrow,
in sickness and in health, to love and to cherish...so
long as we both shall live. This is my solemn vow.

Sarah: I, Sarah, choose you, Terry, to be my
husband, to have and to hold...from this day forward,
for better or worse...for richer, for poorer, in joy and
in sorrow, in sickness and in health, to love and to

cherish...so long as we both shall live. This is my solemn vow.

Scripture Reading

Minister: By inviting a minister to officiate at this wedding, Sarah and Terry invite God into the wedding. But more important, they are inviting God into their marriage. You know, the wedding is but a few minutes; the marriage is for a lifetime. Sarah and Terry have chosen the passage from 1 Corinthians Chapter 13 to be read in their ceremony today. This is a familiar text but is not required reading at a wedding. Sarah and Terry, these words do belong in our ceremony today, but more than that, I hope you will remember these words and read them together throughout the years ahead. Let them guide your love and your life. At the very least, consider reading this text together each anniversary.

The Apostle Paul has written the most comprehensive and compassionate description of love, mature love, enduring love. Often I am asked to read "that piece about 'love is...'" The text, however, begins by telling us what love is not. Let's hear the entire passage. The words are as fresh today as they were 2,000 years ago. Listen for the Word of God:

> If I speak in the tongues of humans and of angels, but have not love, I am a noisy gong or a clanging cymbal. And if I have prophetic

powers, and understand all mysteries and all knowledge, and if I have all faith so as to remove mountains, but have not love, I am nothing. If I give away all I have, and if I deliver my body to be burned, but have not love, I gain nothing.

Love is patient and love is kind; love is not jealous or boastful, it is not arrogant or rude. Love does not insist on its own way, it is not irritable or resentful; love does not rejoice at wrong, but rejoices in the right. Love bears all things, believes all things, hopes all things, endures all things.

Love never ends. As for prophecies, they will pass away; as for tongues, they will cease; as for knowledge, it will pass away.

When I was a child, I spoke like a child. I thought like a child, I reasoned like a child. When I became an adult, I gave up childish ways. For now we see in a mirror dimly, but then, face to face. Now I know in part; then I shall understand fully, even as I have been fully understood. So faith, hope, love abide; these three. But the greatest of these is love.

Are there rings to be exchanged? [If there are children present, I often invite them to stand with me to see the rings and remain for the prayer that follows.]

Rings are not about possession or ownership, they are about commitment. Rings are reminders of the sacred promises you have just made to one another. They are a reminder of promises kept. Rings are the ancient symbol of covenant. Of love. These rings are the outward and visible sign of an inward and spiritual grace. Until this moment, these rings were jewelry chosen by you. From now on, they are your wedding rings blessed by God.

The rings are the perfect circle; they have no beginning, they have no end. As we just heard in the reading of scripture, love never ends.

Please pray with me.

Holy God, we ask you to bless these rings, that those who give them and those who wear them may live in your peace, in peace with one another, and continue in your favor all the days of their lives. Amen.

Exchange of Rings

Terry: Sarah, I give you this ring ...as a sign of my vow... that with all that I am... and all that I have... I honor you. And I will love you forever.

Sarah: Terry, I give you this ring... as a sign of my vow... that with all that I am... and all that I have... I honor you. And I will love you forever.

Minister: Sarah and Terry, you have declared your desire to enter into holy marriage before God, your friends, and families. You have joined hands and spoken your promises to one another. You have exchanged rings.

May God confirm your covenant and fill you both with grace. From this day forward you are husband and wife.

The Blessing

Minister: Sarah and Terry, you have received the blessing of family and friends, now receive the blessing of God.

May God bless you and keep you.

May the sun of many days and many years
   shine upon you.

May the love you have for one another grow and
   deepen and hold you close.

May your dreams come true, and when they
   don't, may new dreams arise.

May you be able to look at one another and say,

"Because of you, I have become the person I
   longed to be."

God Bless! God Bless!

In the name of God the Creator, Christ the
   Redeemer, and the Love and Power of the Holy
   Spirit today, tomorrow, and forever.

Amen.

The Wedding Kiss

*Minister: Friends, please greet Sarah and Terry...
husband and wife.*

****

Jill and Mike

Jill and Mike planned everything they would
say, every word their guests would say, and every
word I would say. Each guest was provided a written
program; every detail was carefully planned. Portions
of their ceremony are included here.

Minister: Jill and Mike, nothing is easier than
saying words, and nothing is harder than living
them day after day. What you promise now must
be renewed and reaffirmed tomorrow. You still are
called, each day that stretches out before you, to
reaffirm this precious commitment of marriage to
one another and in all kinds of personal and ever-
maturing ways. We know real love is caring as much
about the welfare and happiness of your marriage
partner as about your own. Real love is not total
absorption in each other; it is looking outward in the
same direction together. Love makes burdens lighter,
because you divide them. It makes joys more intense
because you share them. It makes you stronger, so

you can reach out and become involved with life in ways you dared not risk alone.

The union into which you are about to enter is the closest and tenderest into which a human being can come. It is a union founded upon mutual respect and affection. Your paths will be parallel; your responsibilities will increase, but your joy will be multiplied.

The Exchange of Vows

Mike: I, Mike, offer you, Jill, my strength and my support,
my loyalty and my faith,
my hope and my friendship.
I will trust, respect, and encourage you.
When we argue and are angry,
I will work to bring us together.
And when all is wonderful and we are happy,
I will rejoice over our life together.
I offer my love without condition.

Jill: I, Jill, offer you, Mike, my strength and my support,
my loyalty and my faith,
my hope and my friendship.
I will trust, respect, and encourage you.
When we argue and are angry,

I will work to bring us together.

And when all is wonderful and we are happy,

I will rejoice over our life together.

I offer my love without condition.

Jill and Mike (together):

We will give what is needed—and more.

We will take what we need—and no more.

We are friends and shall remain so.

We are lovers and shall remain so.

We are individuals and shall remain so.

We are partners and shall remain so.

Me, you, and together as one, I a part of you and you of me, sharing

tears and smiles, defeats and triumphs, and all that life confronts us

with, forever growing in understanding and love. My home is with you.

The couple lights a Unity Candle.

All: God, who gives life to all people and meaning to every moment, we pray that Jill and Mike may be faithful to the covenant they have made before us. May the home they establish be a place of peace and love in which all may share. May your grace and love be their constant companions as they walk through life together. Grant to this couple true love to unite them spiritually, patience to assimilate their differences, forgiveness to cover their failures, and inner peace to comfort them even in disillusionment and distress throughout their lives. As they share their total selves, may their vision of a full and meaningful life be enhanced and deepened, may their strength to make that vision real be fortified anew each day through their love, and may a joy in living be theirs now and forever. Amen.

****

Recommitment

Janet and Bill

When Janet and Bill decided to celebrate their 18 years of marriage with a recommitment ceremony, they prepared the ceremony pretty much as they wanted it to be. They wrote my words and their own. I began:

"We all need love. For one human being to love another human being is, perhaps, the most difficult task that has been entrusted to us. It is not trite, therefore, to say that love is necessary for life, no more than to say that food sustains life. Without food, we will die. Without love, we die a death worse than physical death. Do not depreciate the value of love."

Janet made her vow first: "Bill, I chose you to be my husband 18 years ago and today I choose you again, not because it is expected, not because I have no other choice, but because my love for you is even deeper than the day I married you. And I choose you again gladly and without reservation. I promise to love you always, to listen to you, to nourish you with praise, to never take you for granted. I promise to hold you close when you need to be held, to laugh with you, and to always be your safe haven in this life. I will be faithful to you. I will love you truly and joyfully for the rest of my life."

Bill repeated the same words back to Janet, making substitutions where needed.

I asked God's blessing on the rings to be exchanged.

Bill spoke these words as he placed the ring on Janet's hand: "Janet, I give you this ring to reaffirm my love and commitment to you. Let it remind you that I will be here for you today, tomorrow, and always." Janet repeated the same words to Bill.

I spoke the concluding words: "Bill and Janet, as you renew your marriage vows, which united you as husband and wife, I would ask that you always remember to cherish each other. Respect the thoughts and ideas of one another, and be each other's best friend. Be able to forgive and ask for forgiveness when needed. Let your marriage be strengthened by your love and respect for each other."

We ended with this prayer: "O God of Hope and Promise, our hearts are filled with happiness as Bill and Janet today reaffirm their faith and love for one another. Grant that they may be ever true and loving to each other. Temper their hearts with kindness and understanding. Help them to remember to be each other's friend and confidant so together they can face the cares and problems of life more bravely. Let their home be a place of peace and hospitality."

"Bless this marriage, we pray, and walk beside Janet and Bill throughout all the days of their lives together. We pray in Jesus' name. Amen."

A Recommitment Blessing

I like to read this blessing by the Rev. Lynn James, which I found in the book *Wedding Blessings*, for couples renewing their vows.

May the love that you share give you strength
May the life that you share bring you joy
May the dreams that you share bring you hope
May the faith that you share bring you peace.
And wherever you are in your journey through
    life,

May your hearts always find their way home.
Amen.

****

Baptisms and Blessings

Our congregation is not affiliated with any
denomination, nor do our participants join the
church. So when parents ask for a baptism for a baby,
we cannot offer that sacrament in the traditional
way. I have come to realize that most parents really
want a blessing. And that we can do with a ritual
that says, "You are welcomed and loved!"

Stacy attended worship often and was awaiting
the birth of her second child; I suggested a blessing
for her, her 9-year-old daughter, Teal, and the
baby-to-be. The congregation formed a large circle
with Stacy at my side. Teal distributed the litany to
each participant. I read the prayer and Teal led the
response.

A Litany of Blessing
Liturgist: We pray for all God's children
everywhere. We pray for children who are orphaned
by the violent acts of war.

Response: Bless these children, we pray.

Liturgist: We pray for children whose lives are disrupted and dislocated by sickness, unexpected floods, storms, earthquakes, and other natural disasters.

Response: Bless these children, we pray.

Liturgist: We pray for children whose homes are places of chaos, not kindness.

Response: Bless these children, we pray.

Liturgist: We pray for children who are neglected, abused, unwanted, unloved.

Response: Bless these children, we pray.

Liturgist: We pray for children with special needs: the physically, emotionally, and mentally challenged.

Response: Bless these children, we pray.

Liturgist: We pray for the children in our community; for their health, their well-being, their understanding that each is a Child of God.

Response: Bless these children, we pray.

Liturgist: We pray for our worshipping family here gathered and the children we know and love.

Response: Bless these children, we pray.

Liturgist: We pray especially for Stacy, Teal, and the child they will soon welcome into their family.

All: Bless this family and this precious child, we pray. Help us be family for one another. We pray in the name of Jesus who blessed the little children. Amen.

A surprising footnote: Baby Jacob, due within thirty days, evidently felt so welcomed, he arrived four days later! And he is a blessing.

****

Susan, who is known by Murph because of her last name, Murphy, and David chose to speak their wedding vows on Cozumel Island. They were accompanied by 22 friends and family members. The ceremony was traditional, the weather beautiful. We called it "Murph and David's Wonderful Amazing Wedding." Among the guests were the parents of one-

year-old Truman. They asked for a special blessing
for their son on the day after the wedding. On that
Sunday, the wedding party, including bride and
groom, gathered themselves in a circle on the beach
at noon. I wrote the ceremony.

**A Ceremony of Blessing for Truman Memphis
Hollis Jackson**

As the ceremony began, the precious baby was
passed from person to person around the circle, each
holding him with love, beginning and ending with his
parents.

Leader: Truman Memphis Hollis Jackson, you are
a Blessed Child of God. We stand here to proclaim
your uniqueness, your beauty, the joy you bring
to this family and circle of friends. We say to you,
"Welcome! And thank you!"

We pray with thanksgiving for your new life. In
the presence of your parents, your grandparents,
your godparents, and friends, we pray our hopes for
you. Let the people say:

Circle: We pray for God's children everywhere.

We pray for children in our own families: for their
health, their well-being, their understanding that
each is a Child of God.

We pray for the children we know and love. And we pray for children not known to us but known to you.

We pray for children whose homes are places of chaos, not kindness.

Especially this day we pray for you, Truman, that you may grow in wisdom and in stature and in favor with God and the human family.

We ask this special blessing in the name of the one who blesses us all. Amen.

Appendix Two: Religious Wedding Information

Wedding_____   Anniversary/Renewal of Vows_____
                  (If an anniversary, how many years?_____)

Wedding Coordinator_____

Date_____   Day of the week_____

Place_____Time_____

*Date of civil ceremony_____*This question must be answered.

Will your guests know you have had or will have a civil ceremony? _____

By Mexican law, the religious ceremony is required to be separate from the civil ceremony. The religious ceremony alone is not recognized by Mexican civil law.

Bride's full name_____

First or other name to be used in the ceremony_____

Groom's full name_____

First or other name to be used in the ceremony_____

Family attending: Parents_____

Children of bride/groom _____

        Names and ages_____

Faith tradition (if any): Bride_____Groom_____

Special readings requested_____

Phone/e-mail_____

NOTES: Date filed_____

Acknowledgements

So many people have given light and life to this book. I am grateful to my editor, Sherri Alms, whose wisdom and good sense have guided me. I treasure each couple whose stories you have read; they have been sources of inspiration, challenge, and delight. I thank all those who gave unhesitating permission to share their stories and hope those who I was unable to reach will know of my appreciation. I hope I have reflected fairly all the wedding stories in this book; any omissions or errors are mine alone. I'm also grateful to Nita Penfold and the Reverend Lynn James for allowing their written words to be included in this book.

Finally, I want to put into words my gratitude to Eden Theological Seminary where I grew and stretched and deepened my understanding of theology and love for all God wants for this human family that connects us. I am glad, too, if you bought this book because some of your money has gone to support the Seminary. Maybe an endowment for a new class: *Paradise 101.*

Printed in the United States
73701LV00002B/67-69